A History of Bear Lake

A History of Bear Lake

Bob & Anne Deming

Mill City Press

Mill City Press, Inc.
2301 Lucien Way #415
Maitland, FL 32751
407.339.4217
www.millcitypress.net

Printed in the United States of America

ISBN-13: 978-1-54562-223-0

CONTENTS

FOREWORD

S everal years ago, Bob Deming asked me if I thought it might be worthwhile to write A History of Bear Lake since one had not yet been written. He and Anne Deming wanted to document and preserve the important and colorful history of the lake they have lived on and loved for forty years. I encouraged this history and suggested that telling its story through the recollections of the descendants of its early residents might be the best way to do this and would certainly provide an interesting read.

Published authors, uniquely qualified to write Bear Lake's history, Dr. Robert Deming, a retired professor of English and Dr. Anne Deming, a former Psychology faculty member and college president are not only longtime Bear Lake residents themselves but have been active members and leaders of the Bear Lake Association.

Ten years in the making, they have produced herein that "interesting read" indeed not only for Bear Lake and Chautauqua County residents but for historians and casual readers as well.

Helen Piersons
Town of Stockton Historian

PREFACE

E very lake has its story, but the story of Bear Lake had not yet been told. It was time to tell it through the recollections of the families who first lived here, many of whom still do. The emphasis here will be upon its early and later twentieth century residents and their often very colorful stories of life at Bear Lake in those "early days."

The project began in 2007 with the recording of interviews of family descendants or representatives of the families with the longest histories on Bear Lake. Telling their stories, many of them offered old photographs and rare, early Bear Lake postcards to include which helped illustrate Bear Lake's history.

Our ten year journey researching and writing this history was complicated but rewarding, making us even more appreciative of the privilege of living on uniquely wonderful Bear Lake for the past forty years. It is our hope that this book will not only let readers learn what we discovered about its history in writing it, but might even encourage them to trace the histories of their own specific properties to add to that rich local history. As many have already said, all history is local history, but unlike many histories, this one is not organized chronologically. Readers are invited to jump to those chapters most relevant or interesting to them and eventually enjoy reading *A History of Bear Lake* in its entirety. We will look forward to your responses to it and extend our deepest appreciation to the many current and former residents of the Bear Lake Community who not only contributed so much to this book, but who continue to make Bear Lake the treasure that it is.

ACKNOWLEDGMENTS

Many people helped with this history. Among them are Dick Birmingham, Linda Blodgett, Roger Britz, Patricia Cummings, Barbara Less Daniel, Bob Dobbins, Dorothy Dobbins, James Dobbins, Lyn Dee Dobbins, Dave Dorman, Mary Ellen Dorset, Lloyd Fellows, Thomas J. Goodwill, Michelle Henry, Marshall Kelley, Raymond Kelsey, Ken Klocek, Paul Leone, Laurie Less, Judy McQueary, Dottie McQuiggan, Vince Martonis, Karen Martz, Emery Masiker, Emery R. Masiker, Richard Mott, Douglas Nelson, Tom O'Brien, Nancy Persch, Pat Fellows Petsch, Karen Phillips, Bill Pierce, John Pierce, Marion Pierce, Helen Piersons, Bill Putnam, Katy Putnam, Larry Reimann, Doug Shepard, David Snell, Kay Snell, Willy Snell, Ruth Szumigala, Marilyn Tastor, Kim Taylor, Steven Vannier, Walter Waite, Richard Wang and Martha Wiser. Our apologies to anyone we have missed.

CHAPTER 1:
INTRODUCTION

T his book is a history of a small community along the shores of Bear Lake in the Towns of Pomfret and Stockton in western New York told primarily through the recollections of the earliest families who lived here and may still be living there. The Bear Lake community in 2017 is made up of sixty-some permanent and summer residences and two campgrounds, along one main county road, Bear Lake Road, two small side streets, Gilbert and Lawrence Drives, and Muskie Point Road along the southeast side of the lake. Well known for Lake Erie effect snow storms and the severity of winters in the area, permanent residents number only in the teens, a number that easily quadruples during the summer season.

Walking along Bear Lake Road on a warm July weekend in 2017, with many boats on the lake, swimmers in the water, and people on their decks and porches, it is difficult to imagine the area as it was when Native Americans lived here or later when the Holland Land Company surveyed it in the last years of the eighteenth century. At those times, forested hills on two sides led down into the valley of an as yet unnamed glacial "kettle lake" surrounded by a wooded shoreline where Native Americans walked well-frequented paths to fish and hunt. The nearby Village of Stockton was not here yet, nor was its earlier antecedent, the Village of Delanti.

Some of the early natural history of that Bear Lake valley and information about the Native Americans who were here then are described in Chapter 2. How in the late 1790s the Holland Land Company surveyed its two townships, Stockton and Pomfret, and how large parcels of land in both townships were purchased, cleared, and farmed by early landowners are also discussed in that chapter. Many of the early settlers and others who were absentee landowners back then eventually defaulted on their land purchases to be succeeded by more recent landowners, some of whom have familiar names to readers of this history. Detail about the lots around Bear Lake and their earliest eighteenth century owners is included in Appendix B. While historically relevant, this information is quite obtuse and was, therefore, relegated to this Appendix.

This Bear Lake History, as we have said, centers upon the recollections of the families who lived here from the late nineteenth century and starting building cottages along the lake from the 1920s to the 1940s. Many of these families still maintain year-round or summer residences at Bear Lake. Their accounts of the lakes' early days were recorded and transcribed and some supplemented by family pictures or early picture postcards. Chapters 3 through 14 recount these recollections as foundation for this Bear Lake history.

Much of the interview material was so compelling that we decided early on to quote it at length. This directly quoted material is presented in italics throughout the text. When we intruded into quotations to add clarifications, our comments are enclosed in brackets, and where gaps in our information were found, we returned whenever possible to the original interviewees to clarify what was missing. Clarification was done in person whenever possible during the four summer months when we are in residence at our Bear Lake home, or when not possible then via email or telephone.

Every effort was made during the interviewing and transcription phases of writing to preserve the integrity of what was said in interviews. When later or contradictory information was offered, changes were sometimes made, but in every case we tried to retain the tone and substance of the original interviews. Nor did we "correct" them idiomatically or grammatically. Family pictures and postcards were digitally copied and returned. Due to age and condition, the picture quality of some of them was not always optimal but were still worth including we felt.

Chapter 15 was included to detail the history of Shady Rest, a typical Bear Lake cottage, gleaned from its title search, various US Censuses, and anecdotal information provided by the families who lived in it from 1924 through the present. With this chapter as an outline, readers can if they want to trace the histories of their own cottages from origin to today.

Because most of the ongoing history of Bear Lake is derived from its Associations' activities, the Bear Lake Property Owners Association and the subsequent Bear Lake Association are discussed in Chapters 16. Chapter 17 covers other events and issues in its history, while Chapter 18 details the Association's important grant-funded success at controlling invasive weeds with bio controls, a daunting challenge still confronted every year at Bear Lake.

Two short chapters, 19 and 20, on the Camp-in-the-Woods across the lake and the Phillips Brothers Basket Factory on the west end of Bear Lake Road follow. A "Did You Know That?" chapter (21) was added to collect those facts, myths, legends and rumors that surround the colorful life and legacy of Bear Lake. Included in Appendix A is a list of Officers and Directors of the Bear Lake Property Owners Association/the Bear Lake Association since 1949; Appendix B tells more about the earliest landowners around Bear Lake; and Appendix C includes the Maps that are referred to throughout the text.

Despite our best efforts, to check and cross-check it, some information provided by the interviewees or misquoted by the authors may not be accurate. We regret these unintended errors. Hopefully they will be few and far between, and you will enjoy these remeniscences as much as we did.

CHAPTER 2
THE EARLY PERIOD

Natural History: Bear Lake, like its neighbors, the Cassadaga Lakes three miles to its east, is evidence of the continental glacier that pushed up over the Portage Escarpment over fifteen thousand years ago. When that mile-deep glacier receded northward, it left lots of gravel and a very large chunk of ice that broke off, melted and formed a depression to create Bear Lake. Called a "kettle lake," it encompasses one hundred forty-one acres, and is unique in New York State among public lakes because over 70 percent of Bear Lake's shoreline (about four hundred eighty acres) is bog or wetland, providing habitat for beavers, mink and nesting Great Blue Herons. The Lake abounds in bass, predator, pan, and prey fish. Recently, bald eagles were sighted soaring over the neighboring hills and the Lake itself, but no one has yet seen eagles nesting. Eighty-three species of birds as well as sixty-six plant species have been identified here. There are many acres of various types of trees, primarily oak, maple and hemlock. Ownership of the wetlands is privately held in large blocks with some acres in state and county ownership.[i]

Chautauqua County and Western New York: According to Obed Edson in his 1894 *History of Chautauqua County*, Chautauqua County was probably first settled by Native American "mound builders" who, he says, were not, however, the "ancestors of the Indians found here." These mound builders left earthworks, mostly circular, but "tradition can throw no light upon them."[ii] Edson prepared an exhibit on these Native Americans for the Pan American Exposition in Buffalo in 1901 according to Helen G. McMahon's *Chautauqua County: A History*.[iii] Another early investigator of the Native Americans in this region was Arthur C. Parker who did a lot of work on the Iroquois who settled here after the mound builders. Parker was a grandson of the great Seneca sachem (supreme leader) named Handsome Lake. Parker brought together a list of sixty-one Indian sites in the County and was a participant in the excavation of the prehistoric Iroquois village in Westfield in 1927 and 1928.[iv]

An interesting comment about the early Native American area residents is the following, made by DeWitt Clinton, then Governor of New York, in an address delivered to the New York Historical Society in 1811: *"Previous to the occupation of this country by the progenitors of the present race of Indians, it was inhabited by a race of men much more populous, and much further advanced in civilization."*[v]

Neither Edson's nor any other histories to our knowledge, mention any evidence of the Paleo-Indian culture of ten thousand years ago, though Stanley G. Vanderlaan has done much archeological work on Paleo-Indian hunters who lived in what is now Orleans and Genesee counties. Vanderlaan notes (p.179) [vi] that a very rare Paleo cache of eighty-four chert knives and projectile points was found in 1938 near Barcelona Harbor by Stanley McConnell and Ray Frasier of Bear Lake. They are now displayed at the Buffalo Society of Natural Sciences. McConnell kept thirty-six artifacts; Frasier kept forty-eight.[vii]

Chert, a fine-grained, silica-rich microcrystalline, sedimentary rock was used for starting fires and as a raw material for making stone tools. While the occasional flint arrow points may have been found in Chautauqua County, some later made by Emery A Masiker [Chapter 10] and those collected by Ray Frasier, no distinctly Paleo-Indian sites have been identified to our knowledge.

We do know that other Native American tribes existed later in Chautauqua County. The Algonquins and the Hudenosaunee or People of the Longhouse, also known as the Iroquois, were the two main groups living in Western New York by the late 1400s. The Algonquians lived in wigwams while the Iroquois lived in longhouses. There were also the Eries, a tribe of Huron-Iroquois known as the Nation of the Cat, who were defeated in 1656 by the Iroquois and were absorbed into that Nation. The most prominent tribe in Western New York was the Seneca Nation, known as the "Keepers of the Western Door." They dominated this area and along the Allegheny River.

Family and clan organization among all the Iroquois peoples led to the formation of the powerful political league known as the League of the Five Nations. Also known as the Iroquois Confederacy, it was made up of: the Mohawks, Oneidas, Onondagas, Cayugas, and Senecas, and became the Six Nations in 1712 when the Tuscaroras joined the League. The Senecas are organized into eight animal clans: bear, beaver, turtle, wolf, deer, hawk, heron and snipe. Their society was matrilineal, and clan membership was determined by mothers. Mothers still play a very important social role in Seneca society; the Chief Mother is the oldest and most revered woman in their longhouse. But the political leaders of each clan were more often men. The two highest ranking Sachems were the half-brothers Cornplanter (1744?–1834) and Handsome Lake (1734?–1815).

The Holland Land Company Purchases Western New York: In 1763 the whole of Western New York from the Genesee River to Lake Erie was ceded to England by France. This large tract of land, over three million acres, was called Genesee, named for the Seneca word meaning "beautiful valley." In 1786 after the American Revolution, it became part of New York, which could govern it, but it also became a part of Massachusetts, which could sell it, in an agreement worked out at that time. Robert Morris of Philadelphia, the "banker of the Revolution," bought the Massachusetts Claim in 1791 from Oliver Phelps and Nathaniel Gorham and sold it to the

Holland Land Company, a group of absentee landlords and proprietors, on July 20, 1793. But there was a "catch": the previous owners of this immense tract, Phelps and Gorman, had not only defaulted on their payment for 3.75 million acres, at a cost of one million dollars to Massachusetts, but also failed to ascertain Indian title to this tract. All was not completely settled until the Native American claims to the territory were settled in 1797 by the Treaty of the Big Tree. Treaty negotiations were carried out by representatives of the Holland Land Company, Robert Morris's son Thomas, Indian Chiefs and Sachems (Red Jacket, Cornplanter, Governor Blacksnake, Farmer's Brothers and others) and Jeremiah Wadsworth, a representative of the United States Government. The Indians held out for "reservations" which is why there are still three sovereign Nation Seneca reservations in Western New York. However, that treaty signed on September 15, 1797 provided only one hundred thousand dollars for Indian rights to about 3.75 million acres and a reserve of two hundred thousand acres.

The Holland Land Company, established in 1789 by four Amsterdam firms, sent an agent, Theophile Cazenove, to the United States to explore financial developments and to invest in them. Two of the four Amsterdam firms had already made loans to the United States government during the Revolutionary War and joined the four Amsterdam firms. With financial backing from several Dutch banking firms, Cazenove bought 1.5 million acres of the Genesee lands from Robert Morris. The Amsterdam group then purchased another one million acres and optioned another eight hundred thousand acres. The total land purchase, now known as the consolidated Holland Land Purchase, was 3,250,000 acres. Morris had purchased 3,750,000 from Massachusetts for $333,333.34. He kept five hundred thousand acres for himself, known as the "Morris Reserve."

Early Settlement: In 1797 the representatives of the Holland Land Company, through their new general agent, Paolo Busti, hired Joseph Ellicott, along with his brother Benjamin and *"130 more men,"* to survey the 3.25 million acres of their purchase. A main land office was established in 1801 in Batavia, New York; and Joseph Ellicott after completing his surveying duties eventually became a Company sub-agent with offices in Mayville.

When Joseph Ellicott and his surveyors arrived in western New York during 1798–1799, the Bear Lake/Stockton region was within the County of Genesee and the Town of Batavia. The entire area then owned by the Holland Land Company was covered by a dense, hardwood forest, and inhabited by Native Americans. Ellicott's job was to lay out the 3.25 million acres, set out the boundaries of the Reservations, divide the counties into townships measuring six miles by six miles more or less square, and then divide the townships into sixty-four lots (eight miles by eight miles). Ellicott required field notes from each surveying crew which would describe the following: the quality of the land, types of trees (maple, beech, oak, elm, ash), condition of the soil for farming and raising animals, wildlife, and the suitability of sites for roads, town, inns and other commercial ventures.

Ellicott sent out his surveyors in the spring of 1798 with surveyor's chains to establish lots and townships. Each chain was sixty-six feet long (made up of 100 links with a 7.92 inch loop at each end). The townships were to be six miles square, with each lot being three hundred sixty acres (i.e., sixty chains or ¾ mile square). Eighty Chains or 5280 feet equaled a mile. Ten Square Chains equaled one acre. The surveying teams were expected to get the entire job done in one season; but in fact it took two seasons. Each team was made up of six to nine men who worked under the direction of the chief surveyor (who earned three dollars a day); there were two chain bearers, two axemen, two flagmen, two packhorse men—all of whom worked for fifteen dollars per month each.

John Thompson, in charge of the Holland Land Company surveyors, wrote to Atwater Amzi (August 24, 1798) that he had encountered two lakes, Cassadaga, and Bear Lake in his work. The section on "Stockton" by Deloss Putman in Obed's *History* includes this description: *"Bear Lake, on the north border of the town, is one of sources of Cassadaga Creek, and is noted for the number and quality of its fish, as well as the beauty of the surrounding scenery."*[viii] The entire surveying project cost the Holland Land Company seventy thousand dollars. By the 1840s, all the land in Western New York had been sold off to local investors and/or settlers so that, by 1846, all Holland Land Company actions were ended and the Company dissolved.

Bear Lake in Two Townships: The nineteenth century histories of Chautauqua County as well as the twentieth century histories of the Towns of Stockton and Pomfret, show Bear Lake lying within both townships, which remains the case today. In 1804, however, those townships were not yet named. There was a "district" comprising ranges ten to fifteen which became the Town of Chautauque (the French spelling) and then changed in 1859 to Chautauqua, an Indian spelling. The County was divided in 1811 into the Town of Chautauque and the Town of Pomfret. The Town of Stockton was then separated from the Town of Chautauque on February 9, 1821, and the Town of Chautauque name disappeared.

Towns, Ranges & Lots: Holland Land Company records describe this area of western New York in Towns, Ranges, and Lots. The Towns were numbered from north to south, and the Ranges were numbered from east to west. Hence, the Town of Pomfret comprised Towns 5 and 6 and Range 12. The Town of Stockton eventually became Towns 3 and 4 and Ranges12 and

13. There were sixty-four lots in each Town. Curiously, current title searches for properties in Chautauqua County, will still list your property's deed as for example "... part of Lot 50, Town 5, Range 12."

Bear Lake's Lots & Towns: Bear Lake lies in parts of Lots 56 and 48 of the Town of Stockton (in the north sections of the Town) and in parts of Lots 50 and 42 (in the south sections of the Town of Pomfret). Bear Lake outlet which becomes Bear Lake Creek lies primarily in Lot 47 of the Town of Stockton. The Creek was at one time dammed to provide water power for mills in Stockton (known then as Delanti). Bear Lake Creek joins Cassadaga Creek in South Stockton and then joins Conewango Creek which flows into the Allegheny River, which joins the Monongahela River at Pittsburgh and forms the Ohio River, which then joins the Mississippi and eventually empties into the Gulf of Mexico. This is why Bear Lake dwellers like to claim that Bear Lake is the "headwaters of the Mississippi!" since you can navigate by canoe all the way to the Gulf with a lot of portaging from Bear Lake.

Early Holland Land Company records indicate that in November 1809, Hezekiah Vial purchased Lot 48 in the Town of Stockton, around "Bear Lake Corners" (another early name for Stockton before it was called "Delanti), but no actual settlement was made until 1810. Later according to the Preface of Virginia Washburn Barden's *Holland Land Company Sales in Chautauqua County New York* (1990) property (i.e., the lot) was "articled" when sold, whereby an Article of Agreement was given to the purchaser when he had met the first of his responsibilities—"*paid a small sum to register the transaction, paid part of the purchase price in cash, cleared a few acres and planted a crop and built a building.*" *The land sold for $2.25 and $2.50 an acre.[ix] In contrast, lots in the village of Mayville and Cattaraugus Village (i.e., later the Village of Irving) sold for $5.00 an acre[ix].* Property was "deeded" when the purchaser/

owner completely paid for it, or it was "relinquished" when the owner renounced right to it, and "reverted" if the intended owner "disappeared without formality," thereby making the property available to someone else.

Later Settlement: The Big Landowners: On the northwest side of the lake by the end of the nineteenth century, land acquisition around the lake had settled down and, by the 1920s, three large farms dominated the land, each farm encompassing many acres. To the far northwest along Bear Lake Road was the George Cooper (later Lamkin) farm of about one hundred nine acres; to the east, the Kelly farm of about one hundred seventy acres; and in the middle the Pierce farm of about one hundred eighty-five acres, the largest tract of farm land. On the southeast side of the lake was the Clifford Pierce acreage which later included the Camp in the Woods, a YMCA/YWCA camp, just one part of the nine hundred acre farm called Pierce Acres. The two Pierce families on opposite sides of the lake were not apparently related to each other according to their descendants.

Very early in the twentieth century, George Cooper opened his home to summer visitors, boarded horses on his property, and later added cabins referred to on one topographical map as "Cooper's Cabins". When Walter Lamkin married Edith Cowden in 1934, he bought the Cooper farm and built a small development of four cottages, three of which are still there today (York, Haynes, Wiser) along the ridge leading from Bear Lake Road to the lakefront. He also began leasing and selling lots along Bear Lake Road and the east edge of his property, at Gilbert Drive.

Luther Leroy Pierce (known as Roy), whose farm was in the center section along the lake, had the property on the west side of his big house surveyed for subdivision in 1921 by surveyor C. Burton. That subdivision called "Allotment A" provided for twenty-eight lots from his house west to the Cooper/ Lamkin's property line. In 1941, Pierce had another survey done by surveyor James P. Morrissey which allocated thirty lots behind the original twenty-eight, "Allotment B"; and then east of his central property, Pierce had Morrissey lay out nine lots, each being fifty feet wide by one hundred fifty feet deep for "Allotment C." Pierce started selling lots in the 1930s, but did not include the lake frontage from Bear Lake Road to the shore of Bear Lake. That footage was retained until 2013 when Bob and Lyn Dee Dobbins bought the Pierce property and sold the frontage to the individual lot owners opposite it.

The Kelley family has owned farm land on the east side of the lake since early in the nineteenth century. They farmed it as a dairy farm, but eventually sold the whole acreage of one hundred seventy plus acres to the Masiker family who subsequently sold portions to the O'Brien and McQuiggan families. The Kelleys also owned the land along the south east side of the lake (part of the property sold to the Masikers), and the Clifford Pierces owned the land on the south side where the Y Camp was.

NOTE: Much of the information about Native American tribes in Western New York was found through a Google Search. Much of the information describing the sale of Western New York to the Holland Land Company can also be found through the following links: https://en.wikipedia.org/wik/ Holland_Land_Company The Holland Land Company maps are available at http://www.nyheritage.org/newsletter7. A complete description of the Collection of Holland Land Company maps at the Special Collections Department of Reed Library at SUNY College at Fredonia: www.fredonia.edu/library/special-collections/hlc/ErieCounty.pdf. Other sources about the Holland Land Company include Karen E. Livsey's two volumes *Western New York Land Transactions:Extracted from the Archives of the Holland Land Company* (Fenton History Center, 2012), William Chazanof's *Joseph Ellicott and the Holland Land Company* (1972), and Paul Demund Evans. *The Holland Land Company* (1924).

CHAPTER 3
BIRMINGHAM/LESS/ REIMANN FAMILIES

C hapter 3 begins the chapters which form the core of *A Bear Lake History*, the recollections of the descendants of the earliest residents. We begin with the Birmingham/ /Less/ Reimann families, the largest group of related homeowners in the early twentieth century. According to family recollections, Herbert Reimann "found" Bear Lake in the 1920s. The families soon owned many properties along the lake. The information about them was provided by Birmingham and Less descendants, with most of it from Barbara Less Daniels.

The William Birminghams: William A. Birmingham was manager of the Buffalo regional office of the Veterans Administration, directing all veteran's activities (except the hospitals) in the thirty-one western New York counties. He and Laura Reimann Birmingham, who served as Girl Scout Commissioner, lived in Buffalo and later in life in Batavia. They had two children, Richard and Patricia. William bought the "Fairview Cottage" from George Cooper in 1921 as an engagement gift for his fiancé, Laura. At the time it "*amounted to a fishing shack*," according to a family informant.

Laura and William Birmingham

The original Fairview Cottage

Fairview Cottage (now the larger of the Brad and Marcia Sullivan cottages) was built sometime earlier by Cooper, according to family recollection. *"It was literally a teepee, or lean-to, with old logs and no kitchen and a small interior room and two back bedrooms, and it had an outhouse,"* according to a family source. Sometime between 1921 and 1954, the porch was enclosed and the house sided with "novelty" siding made from recycled World War II materials which *"got moldy very quickly."*

The original lot size for Fairview Cottage was forty by one hundred feet, a lot size the seller, George Cooper, used for all of his lots on the row of lots on the top of the ridge that led from Bear Lake Road down to Bear Lake. The cottage was about twelve feet by twelve feet by twelve feet and *"went up to a hip roof and had an unusual door which was inset with buttons that opened to let the air in (like a turn buckle), and 'bats, lots of them."* Cooper apparently had a grand plan to build a little subdivision along the ridge.

The Birmingham/Less property, including Fairview Cottage and the later built Birmingham "Brown Cottage," eventually totaled six property parcels of very different sizes. The William Birmingham children, Richard (known to us as Dick but as Rich by family members) and Patricia (Pat) grew up in Batavia but summered at Bear Lake.

Richard Birmingham and Sue Canon Birmingham: Dick and Sue Canon Birmingham had three children — Barbara, Maureen and Greg — and summered first at Fairview and then at the Brown Cottage. Dick's recollections about the Fairview Cottage begin in 1934 when he was about five. His Aunt Ella Reimann [married to George Reimann], was very strict about learning to swim and kept taking Dick to the "swimming hole" which was down the lake at the Aldrich Cottage [later the Berndt cottage] where the water was deeper than at the northwest end of the lake, where the bay was and still is very shallow.

Dick also remembers the gas pump in front of Lamkins' store [where the Martz cottage is today] that had to be pumped to get gas. When he was about nine, Dick realls reading all of Shakespeare's plays by kerosene lantern taking turns playing various parts with Pat.

In the early years, water had to be carried in two buckets down the road from Cooper's pump on the farm up the hill until an Artesian well was drilled. The well was only a fifty foot well which, he said, was *"unusual for an Artesian well to flow freely at that shallow a depth."* In contrast, the nearby well at Shady Rest, then George Reimann's cottage, now Deming's, was drilled to a depth of seventy-five feet. When the Brown cottage was built for Dick's family, the well connection was extended from Fairview to that cottage.

In 1954 a major addition was added to Fairview Cottage. The framer/carpenter for the project was Billy Reimann (Laura's brother); cement workers, brickworkers, and painters were Frank Less and Dick Birmingham; overseers and measurerers were Frank Less Sr, George Reimann, and Patricia Birmingham. The stones for the new fireplace in Fairview were hauled by wheelbarrow from the neighboring ravine. The addition provided several expansions of previous space: creating a new kitchen, a larger porch, master bedroom and bathroom and two smaller bedrooms on the back.

Uncle Billy on the inside; Frank on the ladder

Renovations to Fairview Cottage

Fairview Cottage became known as the "honeymoon cottage" because several members of the family, including Dick and Sue Birmingham, honeymooned there. The Brown Cottage, which never got a different name, was built in 1962, *"the same year that Uncle Billy Reimann died"* and two years after Dick and Sue married. Billie's carpentry and building skills were sorely missed. But he had been a great teacher for those who did build the Brown Cottage: Dick, Frank Less Jr and Frank Less Sr and Emery Masiker. Billy had a theory: *"you were a good carpenter if you could drive a spike with a hammer in two swipes of the hammer."*   Among the family pictures is one showing Dick and Frank planting a willow, which eventually towered thirty feet above the water at the corner of the property (now owned by the Sullivan family) and is still there.

The Brown Cottage

Dick and Frank plant a willow

Frank and the Kids

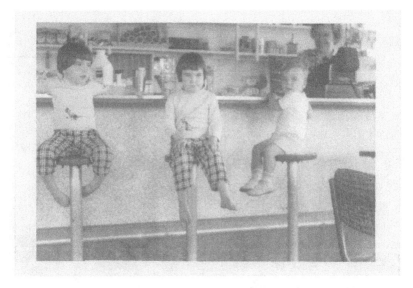

Barb, Maureen & Greg at the Store with Velma Masiker behind
the counter

Another of Dick's recollections was of the telephone service. There were only two telephone lines along Bear Lake Road; one was for Luther Leroy Pierce; the other was for George Cooper (and later Walter Lamkin). At that time, Pierce and Cooper were two of the three largest Bear Lake property owners. Everyone who wanted telephone service had to tie into those two lines in what was known in those days and continued into the late 1970s as "party line" service.

Dick, a graduate of the University of Notre Dame and SUNY Buffalo Law School, spent most of his career at Phillips Lytle in Buffalo as managing partner. He established branch offices of the firm in Jamestown, New York and Wilmington, Delaware. Sue, a former Social Case Worker in Erie County, is a Daeman College graduate. The Birminghams sold the Brown and the White (Fairview) cottages to Marcia and Brad Sullivan in 1994. Sue and Dick Birmingham currently live in Roswell, Georgia.

Patricia (Birmingham) and Frank Less Families: Frank and Patricia married August 2, 1952 and had five children: Laurie, Chris, Kate, Barb and Andy. They summered at Fairview Cottage during the time Frank was stationed in Buffalo for the Navy and worked at GTE Sylvania. Patricia attended Syracuse University, completed a year in Lausanne, Switzerland and became a dramatics teacher at Geneva High School. They moved to Wrentham, Massachusetts in 1969, but every summer until Pat died in 1977, she packed the children into their station wagon along with the two dogs, Sparky and Max, and went to Bear Lake for the summer. *"Frank was an indomitable worker during his many years of visiting Bear Lake,"* Dick said.

Frank Less Sr and his wife Anna were helpful in making the Bear Lake Fairview Cottage a livable space. Frank Sr helped plumb walls and kept books, and Anna was a great cook. Sister Carrie Dziomba, a friend of the family, was responsible for finding all of the screen porch doors from an apartment building being destroyed in Buffalo; they are still in use on both the white and brown cottages

The Reimanns: Laura Reimann Birmingham had one sister, Leona, and five brothers: William, George, Norman, Clarence and Herbert. Clarence died at twenty-seven of a heart problem. Norman died in 1956, George in 1956, and William (who by then was living in Marathon, Florida) lived to be seventy-three. The latter was known in the family as the "strong man."

Leona Reimann, known as Aunt Le,' was born in 1896 and died in 1959. She and her husband Lewis Traub owned the "Pair-A-Dice" cottage down the road from the Fairview Cottage. A white cottage with green trim, it is located at the corner of Bear Lake Road and Lawrence Drive, and is currently owned by the Linde family.

Pair-A-Dice Cottage

Leona worked for the city of Buffalo in the Welfare Department. She married Lewis Traub in 1949 and owned their cottage from 1937 to 1968 when Lewis died. Leona kept journals from 1939 to 1956 which are still in the possession of her niece, Barbara Le' (Less) Daniel and were helpful in this history. Many pages in her journals include only brief date, name, address, and remarks, two to a page, but from them, we learn of the many visitors to their cottage and many family held celebrations there among Reimanns, Lesses, and Birminghams.

William H. Reimann, the oldest Reimann sibling, was a "master carpenter and jack of all trades." He helped frame and build the addition to Fairview Cottage, put on the addition to Pair-A-Dice Cottage and helped replace the windows there. He was the family "go to guy" when things were in need of repair. He was first married to Emma who died in 1949 and subsequently married to Winnie. William died in 1962.

A second journal kept by George Reimann for many years also still exists in the possession of his daughter, Mary Agnes. In it, we learn that he began building the "Shady Rest" cottage (subsequently belonging to the Parrish family and then the Deming family) on August 24, 1924 by clearing brush with his wife Ella (O'Brien). George's brother Clarence, and his wife Kathryn, helped George and Ella build Shady Rest but never themselves owned property on Bear Lake. George and Ella had two children, Robert and Mary Agnes. Pictures of the building, renovations, and other views of "Shady Rest" cottage can be found in the Chapter 15. George's journal was also informative to this chapter and to Chapter 15.

Herbert Reimann, "who found Bear Lake in the 1920s" was married to Ardele Fountaine. In the 1930s they owned "I-Del-Ours" (idle hours), a house he had built across from the Basket Factory (now Cliff Couchman's property) down the lake toward Brocton. They had five children. When Ardele died of breast cancer in 1940, the property became part of a turkey farm. Herbert later married Eleanor Bills. They moved to California in 1957 where he died of a heart attack in 1960.

Herbert Reimann and the Turkey Farm

Clarence Reimann, another sibling, and Kathryn had four children and although they helped build cottages for their relatives on the lake, they never lived on the lake themselves.

In a recent Facebook posting, Larry Reimann recalled that *"As kids we all had to swim across the lake before we could go out to the Lamkin's raft to swim and play* [opposite Lamkin's store, where the Johnston cottage now stands]. *A sugar daddy sucker at the Bear Lake Store and all day swimming, and we were good until supper. The raft was out in the lake from the shore about one hundred yards."*

None of the Birmingham, Less or Reimann families currently live on Bear Lake, but they keep in touch with the Demings, the Johnstons, and others. They were pioneers in the development of the Bear Lake community. Dick was a long-time President and officer of the Association. The Birminghams took possession of Fairview and the Brown Cottage officially on July 7, 1954, and sold both cottages and the surrounding land to Brad and Marcia Sullivan on November 9, 1994.

CHAPTER 4
THE BOGNER/O'BRIEN/ MCQUIGGAN FAMILIES

M any of Bear Lake's early residents were related to each other like the Birminghams, Lesses, and Reimmans in the last chapter. The Bogner, O'Brien and McQuiggan families are among them. Judy Bogner McQueary's father Warren and mother Margy, her sisters Peggy, Sandy, and Jeanne, her uncle Herb, her aunt Dorothy, her cousins Tom and Dottie, Judy's son Mike, and her grandparents have all spent summers at Bear Lake. Judy was one of our interviewees for this chapter as well as her cousins, Tom O'Brien and Dottie O'Brien McQuiggan, Tom's sister and Judy's cousin. For clarity, and to keep them distinct, each family's story is told separately within this chapter.

The Bogner Family: The earliest of this family's visitors to Bear Lake were John and Emily Salzman Bogner, the grandparents of the current residents Judy, Tom, and Dottie. John and Emily rented a cottage on Gilbert Drive. The grandchildren were not sure of the exact date but probably in the 1930s.

Bogner grandparents' cottage on Gilbert Drive

Postcard of Herb Bogner cottage

Next their son Herbert and his wife Ethel Girr came to Bear Lake. Another son, Warren and his wife Margy (Margaret) Morgan came in 1941, but did not start building their cottage until 1948, having purchased the property in 1947 (Lots 8 and 8 E) from LeRoy Pierce. The third Bogner brother, Jack, did not own a cottage at Bear Lake, nor did the Bogner sister Violet who moved to California.

Judy Bogner McQueary: Judy grew up at her uncle Herb's cottage [on the west side of where George Clever lives now] down the lake from the Warren Bogner cottage until her dad built their cottage. Both cottages are still there and used every summer. Judy remembers fishing in Bear Lake with her friend Betty Ebeling, helping her dad build their cottage, playing with her cousins Dottie O'Brien and Marion Bogner and friends Mary Anne Frasier and Judy Shoemaker. She also remembers that at one point in the 1950s, probably after her aunt Dorothy Bogner McQuiggan purchased the corner lot at Bear Lake Corner—the junction of Bear Lake Road, Kelly Hill Road, and Bacheller Hill Roads—an ice cream stand and drive-in were erected there. There's a picture of the "Bear Lake Drive-In" in the Stockton Town Picnic brochure for its sixty first year August 23, 1958, and Judy identified the back end of the car on the left of the picture as her father's, Warren's, car.

There is also a picture of the Warren Bogner family in front of the neighboring Case Cottage "Bear Harem."

Warren Bogner and Margy in the back row;left to right Peggy, Judy,
Sandy in Jeanne's arms

BEAR LAKE DRIVE-IN
Featuring — HOME MADE ICE CREAM
½ Gallons made all year 'round · Super Milk Shakes · 10 Flavors
Charcoaled Hot Dogs · Pizza Pie · Curb Service Fri. & Sat.

Bear Lake Drive-In, 1958

In this chapter and in other chapters, Bear Lake descendants discuss in detail LeRoy Pierce and his "hotel," the largest house on the lake, discussed in Chapter 12. Judy explained that she spent a lot of time at the Luther LeRoy Pierce house, playing with Judy Shoemaker, staying overnight, and wondering about all the jars on the Pierce kitchen table. *"I was fascinated with that."* [Dottie McQuiggan, Judy's cousin, has a similar memory of all the jars on the kitchen table. On the big round kitchen table were jars of mustard, jelly, etc. and when the girls finished their gum they parked it on top of the jars and always remembered which gum was who's!] Judy also recalls that *"Maude Shoemaker,* [Pierce's housekeeper and mother of Judy and Phyllis Shoemaker] *came home from working at the Basket Factory and slopped the pigs. On Saturday, Maude would take us to Brocton for shopping."*

She also has a vivid memory of Mr. Pierce who *". . . sat in that window, on a rocker. We'd sit next to him, and he'd tell us stories. My favorite was that there was an Indian princess buried outside the Basket Factor* [where Cliff Couchman's garage is now]*; and Judy and I would always want to find her burial site. He also told a story about an Indian princess who drowned in Bear Lake, and her father put a curse on Bear Lake.*

I was about ten or eleven when I started visiting the Pierce house. Judy [Shoemaker] *and I shared a birthday. We stayed on the first floor. Phyllis stayed on the second floor. Our mattresses were straw. We'd slide down the bannister. There was a formal parlor--we didn't go in there; you could go through it but not play in it—a huge living room, an office, Judy's mom's room, a big kitchen and a big bathroom. Mr. Pierce's bedroom was on the first floor. So was Maude's. Only Phyllis was on the second floor. There was another room off the kitchen near the bath which had a lot of books in it. I think that was Mr. Pierce's room. He'd be in there smoking his pipe. It was a wonderful place to play. Minnie, Mr. Pierce's wife, died in 1934, and he lived alone for twenty years and never remarried. There were chickens outside. There was a water trough with water from a spring pumped in. They had indoor plumbing. Maude was very kind to me, always showing me things. Maude was never married. She had family outside Stockton that we used to visit. Judy's and Phyllis' father was never spoken of.*

Judy and I became friends in the early 1950s. My mom [Margy] *used to get eggs and milk from the Pierce farm. We went down there one day for Mr. Pierce's birthday. There was an orchard at Pierce's* [on the east side of the Pierce house]. *People would come and buy ice cream and sit in the orchard to eat it. I remember that the farm had an ice house, a cow barn, and a chicken shack. Also the Bear Lake Picnic was held there. He was a member of the Bear Lake Property Owners Association founded in 1949. I remember the water being drawn out of the Lake. Everyone talked about it and that Brocton was taking it."*

Judy was shown a postcard which, like many of the old Bear Lake postcards our interviewees owned, had probably been purchased at the Lamkin Store sometime in the past. On the front of the postcard there was a Bear Lake scene with the typical "Bear Lake, N.Y." written in white script on it. When asked if she could identify the people in the postcard, Judy enthusiastically replied: *"that's Dottie's mother* [Dorothy Bogner O'Brien], *who is also my aunt, my Bogner grandmother* [Emily Salzman Bogner] *and my Uncle Jack* [Bogner, who was Herb and her father's, Warren's, brother]."

Emily Bogner, Dorothy O'Brien, Jack Bogner

Unfortunately, the identity of the photographer(s) and producer(s) of the postcards remains unknown though the authors suspect many could have been by either Russell McLaren or Howard Blanding, local photographers at that time.

Tom O'Brien: Asked about his early years at Bear Lake, Tom explained that he *". . . came up as a kid and stayed at Herb Bogner's* [his uncle's] *cottage, and at a couple of cottages rented from Walter Lamkin on Gilbert Drive. Herb bought his place in 1939. Uncle Warren Bogner's* [Judy's father's] *place was built after World War II.*

I spent all summer out here; a number of summers spent with my cousin Herb Junior who was the son of Herbert Bogner and was called Skip; he also had a sister, Mary. Uncle Jack Bogner had four sons, but we didn't see a lot of them because they didn't spend a lot of time up here.

On top of the hill there, one hundred eighty degrees from the water, was an open field. [referring to the hill above Pierce's farm where there were no trees only hay fields]. *My uncle*

Warren and I would help Mr. Pierce cut and bring in hay from that hill and put it in his barn."

View from the top of Pierce's hill

Tom affirms that the Warren Bogner house was the first cottage built east of the Pierce farm, and the Frasier house [now the Martz house] was the first house built east of the Pierce farm. Going west between the Warren Bogner house and the Pierce farm, there was nothing but a field. "*All we can see now* [along Bear Lake Road] *was built subsequently. My uncle told me once that he could have had everything from Pierce's house to his for $5,000. He started building his house (I was ten or twelve at the time) in two stages. My job was pulling the nails from boards they threw down to me.*

I remember they tapped into the spring behind the Frasier house [now the Martz house], *which is still there. Everyone tapped into it.* [It runs behind the Martz and the former Berndt's houses now.] *The pipe went over to the milk house at the Pierce farm.* [There is] *only one spring up there, and it still runs.*

32

Pierce had an ice house, and they would cut the ice from the lake in the winter and store it in the ice house with straw insulation. At Pierce's farm, the ice house was on the right in the back; the barn and milk house on the left. Down the road, in the front of his house, Mr. Dick Wolf had a concrete box with a pipe sticking out from the bank, and we got our drinking water from there. [Wolf's cottage is on the west corner of Bear Lake Road and Lawrence Drive.] *Eventually the water from the spring was piped into Herb Bogner's kitchen.*

"*We used to go up in the cupola* [of the Pierce house] *and kill bats. Maude Shoemaker would give us a piece of pie. Bobby Rinehart most of the time used to come up and visit, and he is somehow related to Judy (on her mother's side). We were middle teenagers, hanging around, fishing, going down to Maude's. We both had a crush on the older daughter, Phyllis* [Shoemaker]." Tom also recalls that where the Masiker store was later built "*was all swamp, and old Emery came and filled in the swamp and drained it.*"

Asked if the land between Bear Lake Road and the lake itself was clear at the lakefront, Tom said "*No, all brush; couldn't get through. Uncle Warren tried to clear it out over a few years; cut it down and pulled it out. Couldn't get through the brush easily; but could get through to swim. People would drive in to wash their cars where the ramp was. Don't know how the ramp got there, the one that still exists in front of what was until recently the Green cottage.*" [A second ramp on Bear Lake would have been on what is now Szumigala's property where the town line between Stockton and Pomfret continues across the lake to Gravel Point where the former Y Camp was. This was not the ramp currently on Masiker property.]

Tom's other memories included: "*Eddie Gilbert and Bob Siebert and I and a couple of others played baseball down where the Brocton watershed sign is now. Maybe Skip (Herb Bogner Jr.) played; we played regularly, whoever happened to be around. Swam a lot. Didn't go to the Y Camp. Would swim over there after or before camp was in session.* [We] *Didn't fish much;* [but] *hour after hour rowed my grandfather around and around the lake fishing for muskie. Didn't catch many as I recall, but did catch a lot of big turtles; made turtle soup from them. Mr. Lamkin actually made the soup. Can't remember catching muskies.*

Rowed boats around for hours; stayed at Warren's house; rowed the boat down to Lamkin's store, bought something, rowed back. A lot easier to walk but it gave us something to do. Put the boat down at the ramp; pounded some posts in and put a dock in. All mud down there. I can remember when Uncle Warren got his first motor. 5HP motor. Greatest thing since laced shoes!"

The O'Brien family acquired multiple properties on Bear Lake. Tom's mother, Dorothy Bogner O'Brien, had married Matthew O'Brien, and had her three children, Tom, Dottie and Dan. She bought the Masiker farm up Kelly Hill Road as well as a strip west along the north side of Bear Lake Road that went from the corner west to fifty feet east of Maude Shoemaker's house. Tom also talks about his family operating an ice cream stand and store on the lake. [Also mentioned by Judy Bogner McQueary above.] Tom said that at first they operated the ice cream stand at Bear Lake Corners; then a block building was constructed behind the stand which became a store. Tom recalls that during the winter months, the ice cream was made in the big farm house, where Dan O'Brien currently lives on Kelly Hill Road. Later, the store was converted into a home for his mother, who at that time was Dorothy Case. The ice cream stand, featured in a Stockton Town Picnic brochure picture [see picture above in Judy Bogner's account], was moved to the back of the property, where it can still be seen on Joe McQuiggan's property at the corner of Bear Lake Road and Kelly Hill Road.

In 1973, Tom bought the corner lot and the land on the north side of Bear Lake Road from his mother's estate, and at the same time his brother, Dan O'Brien, bought the dairy farm on the north side of Kelly Hill Road. Tom added four bedrooms to the back of the store; and the place stayed as a store until Emery and Velma Masiker built their store farther west on Bear Lake Road.

In 1992 when he moved to Florida for winters, Tom sold his property to his sister Dottie McQuiggan's son and his nephew Joe McQuiggan. Later, moving back to Bear Lake, he bought the former Ethel Sayback house on Bear Lake Road with his wife Marce in 2000.

Dottie O'Brien McQuiggan: Just to review, Dottie is Tom and Dan O'Brien's sister, and their mother is Dorothy Bogner O'Brien. Growing up, Dottie, like Tom, also stayed at her uncle Herb Bogner's cottage or at her uncle Warren Bogner's, which was Judy Bogner McQueary's father's cottage.

O'Brien Children: left to right, Tom, Dottie, Dan and an unidentified friend

After high school, Dottie married Joe McQuiggan, and they had six children: Joe, Katie, Jim, Crissy, Tina and Tom. When her mother (Dottie Bogner O'Brien McQuiggan) deeded her property to Dottie, she kept the fifty foot lot next to Maude Shoemaker's house; and when Dottie sold the house next to her son, Joe McQuiggan, Dottie kept that fifty foot lot, now Fiegel's.

Dottie's current cottage at Bear Lake had previously belonged to Maude Shoemaker, housekeeper to Luther Leroy Pierce. That house, on a fifty foot wide lot, was built by Emery A. Masiker in 1950. According to Dottie, the house was in bad shape when she bought it after Maude died, because Maude had had twelve cats living in it. [The authors remember that that house was known on Bear Lake as the "Cat Lady's house."] It was very small with just a kitchen, a half bathroom, and a sitting room/bedroom. Dottie later extended it to five big rooms.

She recalls that her daughter Crissey was living in the house next door when *"she found Maude dead one day. Crissey would come home from work and bring Maude's mail and newspaper up to her. Crissey started feeling strange as she was walking up to the house. She had a feeling that something was wrong. She pushed the door open, went in and Maude was on the floor, with her dog next to her. Crissey ran over to the* [Masiker] *store and called 911. The dog would not let them* [the emergency personnel] *in. Crissey came back in and contained the dog."*

Like Judy and Tom had, Dottie also shared her recollections of Luther LeRoy Pierce. *"He had a chair in his bay window where he enjoyed his pipe and magazines and books and crossword puzzles."* Dottie remembers that she would wave to him and that he had all white hair. When Maude Shoemaker moved in as Pierce's housekeeper, while also working at the Basket Factory, she brought with her her two daughters, Judy and Phyllis. *"The Pierces had a living room/sitting room with beautiful red velvet furniture. People would come up from Fredonia to rent rooms there, and five or six bedrooms; we slept in bunk beds. He sold ice cream and people sat in the orchard. Bats would swoop down from the widow's walk, probably fourteen or fifteen at a time."* He died much later than his wife Minnie Blodgett Pierce who died in 1934.

Luther LeRoy & Minnie Pierce house

"I remember him sitting there in his chair in the window, Dottie recalled. *I used to go in to talk to him. He reminded me of my grandpa. He was very sweet. I didn't know him hardly at all. I waved to him sitting there. I only remember him sitting there. Maude milked the cows and made pies which she would sell. I remember my grandmother buying them; and they had some chickens running around.*

When you're a kid, you don't pay attention. What did amaze me was that they had this big round table in the kitchen and on it jars of everything. jelly, mustard etc. The girls would be chewing gum, and they'd take it out of their mouths and put in on top of one of the jars. And the jars were covered with gum on this table and they knew whose gum was on which jar."

Dottie now she lives with one of her daughters, Katie, in her Bear Lake House.

The Bogner/O'Brien/McQuiggan extended family, like the Birmingham/Less/ Reimann family owned many of the residences on Bear Lake and still do.

CHAPTER 5
ELIZABETH CROCKER

E lizabeth Crocker died at age one hundred four on May 14, 1999 after a suitably long life, one might say, for an historian. This chapter focuses on her as one of the most prominent members of the Bear Lake Community. Her father and mother, Silas T. Crocker and Ella M. (Stone) Crocker, had a cottage on the lake side of Bear Lake Road which she then inherited (currently the Redden's property), and her brother had a cottage on the land side of Bear Lake Road (where the Cliff and Marie Couchman house now stands). Elizabeth Crocker was Secretary of the Bear Lake Property Owners Association from 1953 to 1966, a record thirteen years. She was also Town of Pomfret Historian and the first Chautauqua County Historian, appointed in 1965, and she served for thirty years.

Her parents Silas and Ella Crocker were married on September 10, 1890 and lived first with Ella's parents at 131 Center Street, Fredonia. Silas was working as an insurance agent, and by 1898, he was a traveling salesman; and the family lived on Green Street. Still later, Silas and Ella and their young children, Lewis and Elizabeth, moved back into 131 Center Street with Ella's mother Sarah. When Silas died on December 21, 1927, Lewis Crocker moved back into 131 Center Street as did Elizabeth return there some years later.[x]

Elizabeth graduated from the elementary curriculum of the Fredonia State Normal School in 1916 and went on to get a B.S. and M.A. from Wayne State University while teaching physical education and health courses in the Detroit school system. Douglas H. Shepard a former colleague of the authors at SUNY Fredonia in a wonderful piece entitled "131 Center, Fredonia" provided much of the information in this Chapter. According to Shepard, *"Elizabeth Crocker returned to Fredonia in 1944 and continued teaching locally, at the same time working with her mother on local history and genealogy . . . It was in the 1960s that she wrote a series of articles for the Fredonia Censor, which was then issued in five pamphlets called Yesterdays in and Around Pomfret. . .After her mother's death, she continued to live at 131 Center Street... ."*And she regularly visited her Bear Lake Cottage.

According to her obituary in the May 18, 1999 *Buffalo News,* in 1975 the Zonta Club of Dunkirk-Fredonia declared Elizabeth Crocker Day, honoring her as one of the first women of the year. In 1979, a particularly auspicious year for Ms. Crocker, she received a Certificate of Commendation from the American Association for State and Local History at its annual meeting in Tucson, Arizona. In the same year she served as Editor of the *Fredonia New York Sesquicentennial Souvenir Historical Book, 1829-1979* published in Fredonia by the Pioneer Press which included her chapter on the "History of Fredonia." She also received the American Legion Americanism Medal, was an Honorary member of Fredonia Grange #1, and a named life member of Trinity Episcopal Church.

Back to her cottage, in May of 1924 George and Eva Cooper (discussed in Chapter 15) gave Silas and Ella Crocker a warranty deed to a cottage lot (fifty-four feet on the water, fifty-three point four feet on the road and one hundred twenty feet deep) directly on the lakeshore. This lot was then conveyed to Elizabeth on July 1, 1925. They are probably the first deeds, as opposed to leases, granted by Cooper. This lakeside cottage was called "White Bear," a name chosen by her mother. The cottage had a beautiful stone fireplace which, reputedly, "burned wonderfully."

A postcard showing Elizabeth Crocker's White Bear Cottage

Her brother Lewis purchased a cottage on the land side of Bear Lake, across and down from his parents'/sister's on the lake side of Bear Lake Road. Lewis also owned a cottage on Cassadaga Lake.

One of the persistent myths at Bear Lake is that the lakeside Crocker cottage had been dragged across the lake from Pierce Acres during one winter. Not so! A different building that Elizabeth and her mother stayed in at Pierce Acres (across the lake) was in fact that building, and it had at first been an ice house at the Brocton train station, before being moved to Pierce Acres and then dragged across the ice in winter to become the boat livery for the Lamkin Store. It currently is the Johnston cottage. So, although Elizabeth and Ella did live on Pierce Acres in a building that was moved across the lake, it was not the Bear Lake "White Bear" Crocker cottage. The Johnston cottage was the one moved across the ice.

Ms. Crocker visited her cottage off and on into her nineties. Sue Birmingham and Anne Deming would go up to say "hello" when she did and remember her efforts to cut her lawn with a hand clipper that she had bought at a garage sale for twenty-five cents on her way to Bear Lake. She was a character indeed. Years later, due to infrequent use, the Crocker cottage began to deteriorate with the porch tilting toward the water; and the fireplace separating from the wall. After she died, the property was sold to the Redden family from Buffalo who also owned the cottage to the west of the Crocker cottage. The Crocker cottage was eventually torn down due of its fragile and dangerous condition. The Reddens retained the fireplace at first, but eventually took it down as well.

For the thirteen years that Ms. Crocker served as the Secretary of the Bear Lake Property Owners Association, her minutes provided a complete and detailed record of the activities and actions of the nascent organization during some of its most turbulent times. As the current Bear Lake Association historian and archivist, Bob Deming appreciated her for her careful and precise record of that period which was very important to compiling the history of the Bear Lake Association and of the lake itself. The Association history is described in Chapters 16 and 17.

A condensed version of Ms. Crocker's obituary that appeared in the *Jamestown Post Journal* was included in The Chautauqua County Genealogical Society's published list of past members: "*She committed time and energy to helping place historic buildings and areas on the National Register of Historic Places. She also worked to remark the graves of more than 60 Revolutionary War soldiers from Chautauqua County. . . She was proud of the cooperation and accomplishments of the thirty-eight municipal historians who are appointed by municipal governments across the county. . . . She was extremely active in the Daughters of the American Revoluton. . . [and was] the registrar of the local Benjamin Prescott Chapter of the DAR. . . Her colleagues. . . recognized her many times and declared November 1975 as 'Elizabeth Crocker Day'. . . A life member of the Chautauqua County Historical Society since*

1948, she devoted many hours of research at the historical society's McClurg Museum in Westfield . . ." [xi] She is buried in Forest Hill Cemetery.

Certainly important to Chautauqua County, especially to the Town of Pomfret, she is also remembered for her years of service to the community at Bear Lake. Its history was also shaped by Elizabeth Crocker.

CHAPTER 6
THE RAWSON/DOBBINS/ ALDEN FAMILIES

Dorothy Dobbins, sharp as a tack at ninety-one, was very generous with her time during several interviews. Often seen riding her lawn mower on her and Bob Dobbins' properties, she represents five generations of the Rawson, Dobbins, and Alden families who have lived at Bear Lake. Her son, James Dobbins, provided genealogical information that was also helpful to this chapter.

James Rawson, Dorothy's grandfather, born in 1873 in London, England, was a seaman in the British Navy and Merchant Marines before coming to the United States in 1892. In 1894, he married Elizabeth (Lizzie) Kitson; they had three sons, one of whom was John Rawson, Dorothy's father, born in 1898, and two daughters, one of whom was Elsie Rawson, born 1904, who would marry Everett R. Alden.

By 1900, James and Lizzie Rawson had a working farm on the northwest corner of Bear Lake Road and Chautauqua Road, until James decided that farming was not his forte, and, in 1917, at age forty-four, moved to Buffalo Harbor to work as a civilian at the Coast Guard Station. The Rawson family lived in one of the five houses in the Buffalo harbor for the lighthouse keepers, and in the early 1930s he was promoted to Light House Keeper of the South Buffalo Light House. Lizzie Rawson died in March, 1923 at only forty-nine, and in 1924 James married Anna Warren who died in 1955 after thirty-one years of marriage. By this time, James was living in Hamburg, and in 1960 at age eighty-seven, he married for the third time, Elizabeth Dickinson. James died at age ninety in 1963.

James's son, and Dorothy's father and mother, John and Clara Belle Rawson married June 24, 1919, and built a house on the northeast corner of Bear Lake and Chautauqua roads opposite James' and Lizzie's house. That house, however, was never completed, nor did they ever live in it. Five years later, in 1924, that house was moved down Bear Lake Road to the bottom of the hill on the right side of the road. It is still there across the road from the Greystone Nature Preserve at 8531 Bear Lake Road,.

The James Rawson Farm, with the driveway curving up to the house and barns from Chautauqua Road, Bear Lake Road disappearing going west down the hill, and Chautauqua Road going off north to the right towards Kelly Hill Road

Dorothy's mother, Clara Lawson was a local Chautauqua County woman who taught at little schools called "districts" that were named for the families with the most kids in that area. Dorothy describes the Einhouse District, named for the Einhouse family, on Kelly Hill Road around Chautauqua Road and Kelly Hill Road as having ". . . *fifteen to sixteen kids at any one time, from first grade to eighth grade. My father had to take her* [Clara] *by sleigh in the Winter up to the school. One of the Einhouse kids would get down to the schoolhouse and get the wood fire in the stove going so that by the time Clara got there it would be warm enough. She taught eight years* [i.e., 1918–1926] *before I came along."*

His house partially built, Dorothy's father, John Rawson, started working as a machinist at the Buffalo Harbor in 1924–1925, before Dorothy was born. His job was making sure that all the lights in the lighthouses on the Great Lakes were taken care of. He had four or five men working for him. Dorothy describes her father's job as *"a machinist, being a civilian under military rule."* John worked in government service until his retirement in 1947.

Wanting to have a place on Bear Lake, he and Clara bought a lot from Luther LeRoy Pierce and erected an Army tent on it in 1926. Dorothy was born that same year in Buffalo. She remembers her mother telling her about living in that tent that first summer of her life. There was an old dresser in the tent, and in the bottom drawer her mother put a pillow and that was Dorothy's crib.

In 1928, her parents started the original one-room Rawson Cottage which was later expanded and updated until it became a year-round house. Dorothy told us that *"they lived there only during the summers. It was built up on posts; we had to worry about the water* [coming down the hill behind the house?]. *My Dad was a fanatic about coming up to Bear Lake every Friday night* [from Buffalo]. *We even came up in the winter time, and my Dad strung a wire*

Original 1928 Rawson Cottage before it was expanded

down to the lake for lights, so we could go skating. Kids from Brocton and Fredonia came up, and then he built us an old-fashioned bob-sled. We'd make a track up the hill where Mr. Pierce would have his corn on one side and his cows on the other side; and we'd sled down. One time we came all the way down the hill, across the road, and out onto the lake."

The Rawson Cottage/house on July 4, 1936, sitting on the stone wall, left to right, are Cousin Marge, Elsie Rawson, Arnold Mahle, John Rawson

By 1940, the Rawsons moved permanently to the Bear Lake house, and as Dorothy said, *"my father* [became] *a beekeeper; he was one of the largest beekeepers in Chautauqua County.* [He had two hundred hives.] *Spring honey or 'light' honey in the spring; and Goldenrod for the 'dark' honey in the fall. He designed a centrifugal machine into which he put the honey combs and spun the honey out of the combs. He was, remember, a machinist! He bottled the honey and sold it commercially to*

Petri's and other companies. After a number of years, he had enough wax collected from whatever he kept. He and mom and Ceil and Walt Lamkin would take a trip to Ohio where he sold the beeswax."

Playing cribbage, Dorothy remembers, was big at Bear Lake. Her parents were in a club *"and would play once a month at least. The Frasiers were here; Walt and Ceil Lamkin; Velma and Emery Masiker; Don and Helen Piersons. Once they had gotten started young kids came along—Arden and Anne Berndt [that would be in 1956]—so they were invited. They'd call everyone up, because by that time everyone had phones. For the longest time, only Mr. Pierce had a telephone."*

Good friends Walt Lamkin (left) and JohnRawson

Dorothy graduated from Buffalo State College with a Home Economics degree in 1947, the same year her father retired from government service. She started teaching at Cato-Meridian

School in Cayuga, New York in 1947, then taught home economics at Brocton Central School from 1966 until 1976, while earning a Masters Degree in Economics in 1971 from the University of Buffalo. She and her husband, Robert Dobbins Sr., had three sons, Robert Jr., Chuck, and James. All three boys attended the Camp in the Woods, the Y Camp across the Lake, just as their mother had as soon as she was old enough at ten. Dorothy had continued attendance at the Y Camp nearly uninterrupted through high school and later became the Sports Director. She even enlisted a friend, Lois Ebling Pierce, who was an Art Major, to be the Arts and Crafts Director. The girls and boys camps were four weeks, respectively. More information about the Camp in the Woods is in both Chapter 11, the Clifford Pierce Family chapter and Chapter 19, Camp-in-the-Woods/The "Y" Camp.

Other Dorothy Recollections: Discussing the early residents on Bear Lake, Dorothy explained that *"Walter Lamkin wasn't here all the time. Walt was first married to a woman* [Fern Pickett] *who now lives in Jamestown. He had a daughter, Marion, who married a Sharp from Jamestown and had two children, Janet and John. Janet still lives in Jamestown; she was a nurse. John Sharp lives in Washington* [state]*; some years later he hit the Lottery. He bought the cottage and told Ceil she could have life use of it.*

[After] *Walter and Fern divorced, he then met a widow by the name of Edith Cowden whose funds helped him* buy *the original Cooper Farm* [the first Lamkin farm and now the Lanni/Fox farm]. *That's how the Cooper property became the Lamkin property when he married her. Edith Lamkin wasn't here very long. Don't know [the] circumstances of her death. He was a widower again until he met Ceil Herrick, his third wife. Ceil had Mary Ellen when she was forty-four and Walt was in his fifties. Ceil taught school in Brocton. Mary Ellen's husband, Mike Dorset had the oil distributorship; he died of cancer after little Mike was born, less than three years after they married. Mike Dorset Jr had cystic-fibrosis. Mary Ellen Dorset and Dave Dorman then took over the family farm up on the hill* [later the Frame and now the Lanni/Fox farm].

Mary Ellen kept the farm house for a number of years while Ceil stayed down in the cottage. [across from the tennis court on the ridge.] *In 1995 Ceil decided to go into the nursing home in Gerry.*[Mary Ellen lived in the cottage in winters until it was sold to the Yorks in 2014.]

The Cooper/Lamkin/Dorset farm stopped at Gilbert Drive and went up the hill. It wasn't as big as Pierce's. Walt let a Boy Scout group build a camp up the hill on the Cooper/Lamkin/ Dorset acreage."

The Alden-Dobbins Connection: Dorothy explained that *"this Bear Lake area is also part of my family—on the other side of the family—Uncle Johnny* [Mr. Everett Robert 'John' Alden] *married my Aunt Elsie Rawson, John's Rawson's sister.* [Everett Alden married his first wife Henrietta Louise Brown in 1925; they divorced in 1930. They had one son, John, born October 26, 1928.] *Elsie* [Everett's second wife] *went to work as a Secretary and eventually left Buffalo in 1939 and worked herself up to Private Secretary to a company division at Socony-Mobil. She had a chance to be very successful. They met each other in 1940 but didn't get married until 1950; and shortly thereafter bought this place* [the Luther LeRoy Pierce estate] *up here."* The very large Pierce house/hotel was eventually torn down, and John Rawson (Dorothy's father) helped to build the current Alden house in its place, now owned by her son Bob Jr and his wife Lyn Dee.

Elsie died in 1964 and John then married Muriel Elizabeth Groom in September, 1966. He died in January of 1969 leaving his estate to his son John with a lifetime use of the house to Muriel.

'Uncle Johnny' Alden and Elsie Rawson Alden

"Muriel and I did a lot of things together, but we haven't always agreed. The little bit we knew of her—she was from Rahway, New Jersey—and John knew her from there. We knew a lot of friends of Uncle Johnny; we had a real good group of people here weekend after weekend. He was a natural born salesman, lawyer." When Muriel died on January 12, 2010, the Alden property was inherited by Douglas John Alden, Everett's grandson, a California resident.

Robert Dobbins Jr. and Lyn Dee Dobbins bought the seventy-eight acre Everett R. Alden estate from Douglas John Alden and Cheryl Alden in 2010 and later sold their lakefront property to each owner facing it so they could own their lakefronts in front of their cottages. This lakefront property extended from the Alden/Dobbins' house west to Dave Couchman's property. After more than eighty years, the Rawson/Dobbins family continues to live on Bear Lake, Dorothy year round and Bob and Lyn Dee in the summer. They remain an important part of Bear Lake's history.

[Note: there is a picture of the big Pierce house in Chapter 12, the Luther LeRoy Pierce chapter.]

CHAPTER 7
THE KELLEY/KELLY FAMILY

T he Kelley property was the third of the three large farms on the north side of Bear Lake. One of the Kellys, the late Marshall Kelley was eighty-seven years old at the time of his interview on June 23, 2010 in Greenwood Cemetery in Stockton where he cut the grass and killed the weeds around the tombstones. He lived on Stockton Road (Route 380) two houses south of Cemetery Road.

Marshall stopped his mowing that afternoon to talk about the Kellys. He explained that sometimes his family name was spelled "Kelley" and sometimes it was spelled "Kelly." [It appears that the earlier Kelleys used "ey;" and the more recent family members use "Kelly".] Marshall was not sure that Kelly Hill Road was named after his family, but it was likely true. At last count, he said, *"there are nineteen Kelleys/Kellys buried in the Greenwood Cemetery, and there have been many Kelleys/ Kellys around here for over two centuries."*

Marshall Kelly's parents, grandparents, and great grandparents lived along Kelly Hill Road, around Kelly's Corners (also known as Bear Lake Corners), at the corner of Kelly Hill Road, Bacheller Hill Road, and Bear Lake Road, and along Bear Lake Road. His father was Tower Kelley and his mother Frances (Howard) Kelly; his grandmother on the Kelly side was a Monroe; but he could not remember his paternal grandmother's name. On his mother's side, his grandfather was Clarence Howard, but again he did not remember his grandmother's name. [Nor could we find any helpful information about the grandmothers' names in the Greenwood Cemetery.]

The Kelley/Kelly family has resided in this area from September 9, 1810 when Richard Kelley bought one hundred fifty acres on Lot #43 (Township 5, Range 12) from the Holland Land Company, making him one of the area's earliest recorded settlers. Although Richard defaulted on that property, he renewed his claim on February 9, 1830.

Throughout the nineteenth century there are Kelley land records and deeds in the Chautauqua County Clerk's Office, sometimes also mentioning the Turk family since the two families intermarried. The Turk land was immediately to the north of the Kelley land on Kelly Hill Road. On August 15, 1881, according to those records, Maria Kelley, the widow of Franklin Kelley passed on land in Lots #42 and #48 (Liber 160, p. 255) to Carrington K. Kelley and his wife Fanny M. Kelley and to James M. Kelley. The 1839 map shows Kelleys in place along Kelly Hill Road on both the east and west sides of the road below Sodom Road, also called Turk Road, all the way down to Kelley's Corners.

Kelley families also controlled much of the land on both sides of Kelly Hill Road up to the cemetery on Kelly Hill Road and owned portions of the land going up Bacheller Hill Road, and on both sides of Bear Lake Road going south towards Route 380. This included the family home of the "Kelly Brothers" (Ray and Ernest) at 7806 Bear Lake Road currently owned by the Donald Harrington family. Farmland comprised the Kelley land leading down to the lake on the south side of Bear Lake Road; there were no buildings; and the land extended beyond what is now known as Muskie Point Road.

Marshall grew up on the Kelly farm at the corner of Bear Lake Road and Kelly Hill Road (currently the Dan O'Brien farm). He spent a lot of time on the Lake growing up before he went into the Army. In January of 1946 he returned to run the family farm and the Sugar Bush, as he had helped do most of his life up to that point. He had learned how to run the farm from his father, Tower Kelley. Although he did not recall when his family began acquiring all of their land, he did remember that when he returned from the Army in World War II in January of 1946 "*the family wanted to sell the entire property to the Masiker family. I said I wanted to keep the farm (including the cows) and the Sugar Bush. The Sugar Bush was an active maple syrup operation, requiring tapping maple trees in the spring for their sap, boiling it down into a syrup, and selling it to whomever came for it, and also shipping it to friends and family living elsewhere.*"

A year later in 1947, Marshall decided that, although he did like the Sugar Bush part of farming, he didn't like "*the cow part of farming.*" He decided to go ahead with the sale of the entire property to Emery A. Masiker (i.e., the father of the current Emery R. Masiker and grandfather of the current Emery M). After that sale, Marshall helped Masiker with the farm and the Sugar Bush, while continuing his job at the Alco plant in Dunkirk. He also helped him chop out the brush in the swamp created by the creek that crosses the former Kelley property and flows into Bear Lake. By re-channeling that creek, the area eventually dried out, and Masiker was able to begin to build and rent cottages on it facing Bear Lake Road. He also helped Masiker create the channel that leads to the former Masiker/Clever store and the channel that divides the store property from property rented from the Masiker family by the Conservation Club.

"*The Kelly brothers* [Ray and Ernest] *were married to two of the sisters of Marshall's mother, Frances Howard, Ray to Bertha, and they had one daughter, Onale, and Ernest was married to Jesse, and they had one son, Gilbert. The Kelly brothers and their families lived in the same house* [that last house on the left before Route 380 joins Bear Lake Road] *and are buried next to each other, near the* [380] *highway, in the Greenwood Cemetery. The brothers had a saw mill, powered by an auto engine taken from a sixteen cylinder Cadillac.*"

The original Kelly Farm. Later the Masiker and then the Dan
O'Brien farm

The Kelly house at 7806 Bear Lake Road

The property across Bear Lake Road from the Kelly brothers' farm went all the way down to the outlet, and was called the Bear Lake Farm. The brothers only owned the land on the east side of Bear Lake Road going toward Stockton Across the street from them, a swamp was created by the Bear Lake Creek spreading out among the low-lying, brush filled areas leading from Bear Lake Road to the outlet.

Asked what Bear Lake was like when he was growing up, Marshall explained that: *"There was a big hotel* [on the Pierce Farm] *there. I used to go there to get ice cream. There was a little ice cream stand right at the road. Pierce only made vanilla ice cream. He also had a picnic area, and a boat livery (row boats only). Might have had about fifteen boats. Roy Pierce's son had a big boat with a power motor. He was educated and lived in the middle part of the state. He was a chemist. He had a stunted right arm, but still rode a motorcycle. His name was Howard, and he owned a piece of property along Chautauqua Road."*

He clarified that while he was growing up, the Pierce Hotel " *didn't board people there. When Pierce's wife Minnie died, they didn't do anything about the boarding. She was a great person; we'd go in to get a scoop from 'Aunt Min,' and she'd pull the big ladle out. They might be buried in Fredonia. Johnie Alden bought the farm and tore it down. Alden is also buried in the Stockton cemetery."*

According to Marshal, the Kelleys owned quite a bit of water frontage and *"dried up the swamp at Muskie Point, which was not called that then; there was no road running down there. I worked for Masiker to cut that brush out of the swamp, and opened up the creek channel to make an entrance into the lake. Old Emery was good at anything. Made bows and arrows. I used to help him on the farm. Emery had a few cattle, but no one else raised cattle. He didn't like farming. He built cottages on the left hand side of Bear Lake* [going west past the Store.]

He dug the canal (which helped drain the swamp), and dug the second canal as well to help with the drainage."

Most of the large Kelley family has moved away from the Bear Lake area, but their influence and presence is still felt and remembered.

CHAPTER 8
KLOCEK/CASE FAMILIES

K en Klocek swam from the Bear Lake Road side across the lake to the former Y Camp before his Fredonia High School Reunion in 2015. He spent many summers here as a resident, a frequent renter or visitor over the years, and fondly remembers spending much of his childhood on the Lake. His aunt and uncle, Edwin Harold Case and Agatha Blanche (Koplin) Case purchased Lot 6E from Roy Pierce on July 29, 1947. The lot was narrow, and the Cases didn't buy the lot behind their lot. Agatha Case was very active in the Bear Lake Property Owners Association and frequently served on the social committee for the annual Association picnic held at the Sahle's cottage (which was later moved back behind the Fred and Helen Carr's house when it was built) and is now the George Clever house). The lot, he said "was narrow," and the Cases didn't buy the lot behind theirs. For several years, the Cases had *"what they called the 'shanty,' a tall narrow building which housed boats, oars, outboard motors, and 'summer stuff' which sometimes served as a bunk house."* The original Case shanty still exists behind the former Case cottage. After several generations in the family, the Case cottage was sold to the Mogfords in 2014 and totally remodeled.

Matt Klocek in front of the Case Shanty about 1949

After the initial Case cottage was built, Ed Case's father, Fred Case who was a carpenter, came with a surveyor to lay out the piers that served as a more stable foundation. *"Cement blocks were added later, but the house settled once."* Building of the house was, according to Ken, a *"family thing, involving Ed Case, his brother Fred Case (Ken's father), and Ed's brother-in-law, Ed Koplin). Ken's father famously encouraged the workers by offering that if you put in enough nails, you get a key to the cottage, an irresistible reason to work."* The cottage, as a result, became the center of a lot of family activities that had previously taken place at Point Gratiot in Dunkirk.

Behind the cottage was a stream that belonged to Roy Pierce with a spring house on it. The water was piped down the hill to the cottages. The five members of the Klocek family stayed in the shed for a week at a time. But other than those family weeks, Ken and his older brother Matt were mostly day visitors to the Case cottage. When Ken was four, his family rented a cottage up the hill on Gilbert Drive where Walt Lamkin had rental cottages.

As a kid, Ken remembers *"rowing down the lake whenever he had five cents or more. It was a great adventure being allowed to take out a boat and row down the lake by yourself! We didn't walk. The dirt road was frequently oiled to keep the dust down."* His uncle built a huge raft out of fifty gallon drums and anchored it out in front of the Case cottage in deeper water. It had a deck and a ladder and was chained and anchored, and in the fall a chain was put on it, and it was brought it in to the shoreline.

The Kloceks were, as we said, mostly day visitors to their uncle's cottage. In contrast, Ken said *"the Bogner girls lived at the lake for several days or weeks at a time for several years. They have a much different perspective of their time at the lake."* In the late 1940s, the Warren Bogner cottage and the Case cottage were the only cottages from the Pierce's farm to Kellys Corners. There was, however, one house there belonging to the Frasier family. All the rest was farm land.

Both Ken and his brother Matt attended the Camp-in-the-Woods but only for one year. *"I was parked there when my parents went to Canada for better fishing."* The brothers attended the Boy Scouts Camp Merz on Chautauqua Lake. As kids they lived across the street from Harold Duncan, County Secretary of the Chautauqua County YMCA. The Camp was "Duncan's baby." Ken remembers mowing Duncan's lawn when he was ten to save his money to attend the Camp; because it cost $12.50 a week. *"I earned every cent of that myself. If you wanted to go to camp, you had to earn the money yourself. I was a year younger than I should have been* [to attend camp]. *You brought your own bedding and sleeping bag, and slept on iron cots in World War II surplus tents on platforms. In the late 1940s, Town Line Road came off the hill (Bacheller Hill) right into the lake. People drove down that road and washed their cars where the*

road would have entered the lake if it hadn't curved right onto
Bear Lake Road."

Ken joined the Navy in 1960 and subsequently piloted air-
planes for Eastern Airlines all along the east coast; but his fond
memories of his family's activities at Bear Lake continued to
draw him back after he retired. Living in Virginia, he rented
several places on Bear Lake for many summers as did his
brother Matt, who travelled here all the way from Hawaii.

Ken recalled the basket industry that once existed here:
"*Baskets were an important part of the local culture. . . at Bear
Lake and in Stockton itself. Bear Creek was damned up. At one
time on one of the branches of the Creek, there was a saw mill
dedicated to making basket handles. It may have been where
the old Stockton Sales warehouse is. Baskets were extremely
important locally since they were used to pack grapes and other
produce. Grape 'packing houses' were part of all the large
grape farms before Mr. Welch adapted pasteurization to grape
juice. Grapes would be packed in eight and twelve quart baskets,then taken to the rail sidings on the Lake Shore routes
where entire freight cars would be filled with grapes. They were
shipped to the produce markets that could be reached overnight
without refrigeration.*

Coming up with anything written [about Bear Lake] *before
the 1940s is unlikely,"* Ken advised.*" There were not that many
people here, unlike Lily Dale, for example. Bear Lake was just
this place that stored water to fill the Mill Ponds and to run the
mills in Delanti (Stockton). And maybe catch some fish.*

*I recall that the enclave only existed from the north west bay,
where the former Carl Loiocano's house is, now his daughter
Beth Scarborough's half-way down the lake to Pierce's farm.
There was nothing except cows past the Pierce house (except
for Ray Frasier's cottage) on either side of the road all the way
to the four corners. Back at the northwest end of the lake there
was a row of cottages (still there: from Sullivan, through Wiser,
through Haynes, and ending at the road end with the former*

home of Ceil Lamkin) and apparently a boat rental place, as depicted in old photos.

When I was young, there was a store, and somebody must have rented boats on the lake side of the road opposite the store. This would be at the corner of Bear Lake Road and Gilbert Drive; and the Johnston cottage on the lake may have been the boat livery. The store was first operated by Walter Lamkin. There was a concrete wall there, perhaps docks. The remains of that, or another wall, may be visible under water in front of the blue cottage [Johnston's cottage], *or in that area.*

We used to row down from my uncle's place [the Case cottage] tie up there, and buy a candy bar or popsicle at the store, and row back. It seems as though it was a quasi-public place. In the 1940s, and probably before, there were rental cottages up the hill behind the store [on Gilbert Drive]. My parents rented one there during the summer right after the War.

Reflecting Helen Pierson's advice to us, Ken said *"If there is a history to Bear Lake, it is probably only in the memories of folks now living."* We agree with Ken and Helen and hope the memories we've captured from him and others will create that history.

CHAPTER 9
THE LAMKIN/DORSET/ MARTZ FAMILIES

A s mentioned earlier, by the early 1930s there were three large farm owners on the Bear Lake Road side of the lake: the Tower Kelley family (with about one hundred seventy plus acres on the east side), Roy and Minnie Pierce family (with about one hundred eighty-five plus acres in the middle), and the Cooper and later the Lamkin families (with about one hundred nine plus acres on the west side). On the south side of Bear Lake the Clifford Pierce acreage included a six hundred acre farm and the three hundred acre Pierce Acres with the Camp-in-the-Woods. The Kelleys were discussed in Chapter 7, the Roy Pierces will be discussed in Chapter 12, the Clifford Pierces in Chapter 11, the Coopers in Chapter 15, and the Lamkins discussed in this Chapter.

Walter M. Lamkin was the "last" of the big farm owners, not coming into his acreage until 1934 when he and his second wife Edith (Cowden) Lamkin purchased the George Cooper property which had earlier been placed in receivership and purchased by John L. Sullivan. The Cooper family had been in possession of its farm for several generations from the middle of the nineteenth century when John and Dulcena Cooper took control of the property. A more detailed discussion of the Cooper family in Chapter 15 traces their history and what was Lot #50 in the Holland Land Company survey.

Lamkin bought the mortgage from Sullivan in 1934 with money supplied by Edith to whom he was married for only a few years before she died of cancer. He was divorced from his first wife Fern Pickett, with whom he had a young daughter, Marion. At one point, he, Fern and young Marion lived on the corner of Seymour Street in Fredonia.

He had previously owned a body shop in Perrysburg and then another one on Canadaway Street in Fredonia where he made canvas tops for cars. Before Lamkin's purchase, George Cooper had developed rental cottages on Bear Lake Road, referred to as "Cooper's Cabins" on one 1916 topographical map and some additional cottages on Gilbert Drive. Several of the families interviewed for this history mention relatives renting cottages on Gilbert Drive. His large farmhouse also took in boarders during the summer, and he reputedly stabled horses as well.

In 1934, Walter and Edith Lamkin became farmers on that farm land. According to Mary Ellen Dorset, his daughter by this third wife Francelia (Ceil) Herrick Lamkin, *"Walter was a carpenter, but he really was a cabinet maker. He was not a 'finisher.' He would do the cabinets for a remodeling job. He didn't finish anything. He built houses."* Mary Ellen had a piece of Lamkin's business stationary, which listed what he did as *"carpentry, cabinetmaking, and remodeling."* His father and mother, Frank and Mary Lamkin, lived in Perrysburg at the time that Walter and Edith bought the Bear Lake farm; but they lived, for a short time, at the cottage at the top of the row of cottages extending along the ridge from Bear Lake Road to the lakeshore. The Lamkin farm (and its predecessor the Cooper Farm) ran east to Gilbert Drive (the west property line of the Roy Pierce farm), and west along Bear Lake Road for almost a mile. It also went up the hill above the farm. The Lamkins sold off some of the land, where Chuck Haenel now lives, to the Elliott family; and the land where Ken and Mary Ann Balling now live (and before them the Art Clever family) was also sold. The Balling/Clever/Kerns house was built by the Kerns family, and according to Mary Ellen *"the bricks came from the old Depot down in Dunkirk. Every day before they could go swimming, the three sons had to clean off the bricks. So many bricks a day. They had a trailer, and they tent-camped until the house was built."*

View from the top of Lamkin Hill looking toward the lake

Winter view of Lamkin Farm

Lamkin farm in the 1930s

The Lamkin farm was run by Walter's father, Frank Lamkin. It had chickens but no cows, a livery stable for the boarding of horses, and renters in the farm house before Walter bought it. Mary Lamkin had a stroke when her granddaughter Mary Ellen was about a year old. Bedridden, she lived with the Lamkins at the farm so that she could be taken care of. Frank stayed at the farm in the winter, but moved down to the cottage on Bear Lake Road for the summer. He died in the 1950s at the age of eighty-eight several years after Mary died.

According to Mary Ellen, her father *"had a wood working shop at the farm, and he opened the Bear Lake General Store at the corner of Bear Lake Road and Gilbert Drive in the 1940s. That store building was originally a garage moved down from the farm and then remodeled."* The Lamkin's Bear Lake Store apparently stayed open until at least 1954 since there is a picture of it in the Stockton Town Picnic brochure for August 18, 1954. It was later owned by the Hartmans.

"Lamkins Bear Lake Store"

Confections — Groceries — Fishing Tackle
Boat Livery — Cottages

Phone: Brocton 3262   Walter Lamkin, Prop.

Lamkins Bear Lake General Store 1954

"Hartman's Bear Lake Store"

Successor to Lamkins

Confections — Groceries — Fishing Tackle
Boat Livery — Cottages

Phone: Brocton 3313   William Hartman, Prop.

Hartmann's Store (1955)

Lamkin's Boat Livery

A Bear Lake Postcard view of the Lamkin store on the left, Bear Lake
Road on the right, and the driveway to the Lamkin Farm left

The Stockton Town Picnic brochure for the next year, 1955, shows a picture of what was then called "Hartman's Bear Lake Store." Apparently, after he owned the store for a few years, Walter sold it and the boat livery to Bill and Margarite Hartman who in turn only operated it for a couple of years. The Hartmans were related to the Perkins family who built and owned the cottage Martha Wiser now owns. In 1972 the store was sold by Ray Hammett to Norman and Ruth Martz when Gary Martz (the current owner along with Karen Martz), was fifteen years old. Gary and Karen took over the Martz cottage from Gary's parents after it had been converted into a cottage. In 2017 it is for sale at this time. The Martzs have moved to the former Lanni/Fox property down the road and Lanni and Fox have moved into the former Lamkin farm house. Bear Lake people tend to stay on Bear Lake.

Soon after Walter established his store, he met Franceila (Ceil) Herrick, whose parents, Elisha and Lida Herrick, had a cottage directly across Gilbert Drive from the store where the Konert cottage now stands. Ceil Herrick Lamkin grew up in Dunkirk and taught school in Buffalo and in Brocton. After his second wife died, and Ceil had divorced her husband, she met and married Walter. He was already in his fifties and Ceil was forty-four when they had Mary Ellen.

Elisha and Lida Herrick's cottage

"LAMKINS BEAR LAKE STORE", Bear Lake, N. Y.

Confections — Groceries — Fishing Tackle — Boat Livery — Cottages

Phone Brocton 3262 — Walter Lamkin, Prop.

Muskie brought into Lamkin's store to be measured and weighed. Caught by Pete Borst from Brockton. 46" long and 21 pounds

While still running the store, Lamkin added onto the cottage on Bear Lake Road (now the Ford house), remodeled it and continued to rent it when it was not occupied by Lamkins. Mary Ellen and her husband Mike lived in this cottage. In later years, after Walter died in 1972, Ceil lived there during the winter while Mary Ellen and her husband Mike Dorset and their son Mike Dorset Jr lived at the farm up the hill (now the Lanni/Fox home). Mike Dorset died of cancer less than three years after their son was born, and Mike Dorset Jr, born with cystic-fibrosis, also died very young.

Lamkin cottage; Frank Lamkin standing outside

After Walter Lamkin died, the cottage passed to Mary Ellen's half-sister, Marion (Picket) Sharpe and her husband Clifford Sharpe from Jamestown. The Sharpes had two children, Janet and John. Years later, after John won the New York lottery, he bought the cottage. He later moved to Washington State and gave Ceil life-use of it. When Ceil went into assisted living in Gerry, Mary Ellen lived in it in winters, and the Sharpes visited

71

from Washington in summers. It was sold to Bob and Nancy Ford in 2014.

Mary Ellen recalled that there was once a dump at Bear Lake operated by her father. *"It was past the Dotson' on the other side of the street* [on the south side of Bear Lake Road] *just before Eckstrom's house. People paid to dump stuff there. There was a wide spot in the road. Every once in a while, my Dad would go down with the tractor and cover it up."*

She also talked about the Bear Lake picnic grove, the Sahle picnic grove; *"where George Clever now lives, there was a 'picnic grove' behind the Sahle cottage. The Sahle cottage was moved back when the current* [Clever] *house was built* [by Fred and Helen Carr]. *When the Bear Lake Property Owners Association held their annual picnic and meeting, it was often held at the Sahle cottage. Grampa and Gramma* [Sahle] *held the annual picnic. They were not my real grandparents; they were not related. I just knew them all my life."*

Mary Ellen also explained that *"where Cliff and Marie Couchman live is where* [the Lewis] *Crocker cottage was. Elizabeth* [Crocker] *and her mother lived at the lake cottage, next to the* [Ed] *Wolf cottage* [currently the Reddens cottage]. *I was afraid of Elizabeth as a little girl, but I remember Mr. and Mrs. Crocker. My grandfather's* [Herrick's] *front porch was on the corner of Bear Lake Road and Gilbert Drive, and* [Lewis Crocker's] *back door was right there on the next lot. There wasn't much lawn between them. That cottage was also falling down, like the one Elizabeth and her mother lived in on the lakefront."* [Later bought by the Reddens and taken down when it could no longer be restored.]

No Lamkins or Dorsets currently live on Bear Lake, but Mary Ellen lives nearby, and her family is fondly remembered by many here.

CHAPTER 10
THE MASIKER FAMILY

A familiar family at Bear Lake to this day is the Masiker family. Three generations of Emery Masikers have lived here, the first Emery A, the second, his son Emery R, and the third, his son, Emery M. Most of the Masiker family history was taken from several recorded interviews with Emery R, his brother Bob and Willy Snell, friend to several generations of Masikers and son of William and Mabel Snell, formerly of Sodom Road

Emery A. Masiker and a brother, Emmett, came to Bear Lake from Pittsburgh when Emery was "*about seventeen, Emmett about twelve.*" Emery R explained they were brought to Bear Lake after their parents died when they were quite young, leaving Emery A, Emmett and eight other brothers and sisters. Emery A was born in 1907 in Gastonville, PA. Apparently, a church in Pittsburgh made connections to "*farm these kids out*", According to Emery R, and "*find homes for them.*" When they arrived at Bear Lake, they lived at the Snell family home on Sodom Road (as mentioned earlier, Sodom Road ran between Kelly Hill Road and Fredonia Stockton Road, and was also known as Turk's road, named for the Turk family that owned property along Kelly Hill Road). Remnants of Sodom Road still exist today.

William S. Snell and his wife Mabel A. Snell lived on Sodom Road from the early 1920s, around the time the Masiker brothers arrived in 1924. The teenage boys helped the Snells, along with John Rawson and Walt Lamkin, build the original building at the Snell Basket Factory on Bear Lake Road (on the current Cliff Couchman antique automobile restoration property); but the boys did not work at the factory, according to Emery R. For their board and keep at the Snells, they worked at the Tower M. and Frances Kelley farm on Kelley Hill Road (currently the Dan O'Brien farm). Willy (Willis) Snell (now deceased), a younger teenage contemporary of Emery A and Emmett, remembered Emery A as being called *"the old Chief."*

Emmett married Martha Johnson and built a house across the road from the Snell's basket factory. That house was next sold to Emmett, Jr, and later to its current owner, Dick McCloskey. Emery A built a second place east of it on the same, south side of Bear Lake Road next to Herbert and Ardele Reimann's cottage, "I-Del-Ours," which was built in the 1930s. That cottage became a turkey farm after Ardele died of breast cancer in 1940. (See a picture of the Turkey Farm in Chapter 3.) Emmett built a third house (now the Dotson house) on the north side of Bear Lake Road, between the skeet shooting range (now on Mogford property) and the Lamkin farm. The Masiker brothers worked at Bear Lake until World War II began; younger brother John joined them in the late 1920s, but apparently never had a house of his own at Bear Lake.

Emery A moved back to Pittsburgh in the 1930s to work at the Heinz factory, married Velma Michel on September 12, 1939 and had three children, Bob, Emery R, and Margie. He was exempt from military service because of his watch repair job. He also worked in a toy factory (a wood working operation), but did watch repair all his life.

The Emery A family eventually decided to return to Bear Lake, according to Emery R. They wanted to purchase the Kelley family holdings, about one hundred seventy plus acres that ran up Kelley Hill Road almost to Sodom Road, up Bacheller Hill Road to the forest area, and along Bear Lake Road from the four corners west to property owned by Leroy Pierce and east to what is still the Campbell property. This substantial purchase was made possible because neither of the Kelley sons was interested in continuing the farm. One son,

Marshall, had gone off to the military, and Emery R was not certain that another brother, Jimmy, was at Bear Lake when the Masiker family returned to the area in about 1945. Emery A wrote to the Kelleys, asking if they wanted to sell the place, and they, in turn, contacted Marshall to ask him if he had any interest in it. At first he was not interested and wanted to keep the

Emery R and Bob on a "horse" at Kelley's farm

farm. But eventually the next year the Kelleys sold the entire property to the Masikers on April 30, 1946.

After the purchase, Emery A, Velma and the three kids lived in a cottage behind the Kelley farmhouse while they enlarged

Emery R and his Pet Crow 1948

it. They worked as dairy farmers from 1946 to 1958, while preparing to move into their planned store across the street. Emery A still owned the small lot and house on the southwest side of Bear Lake Road, discussed above, but the Kelley Farm was the family's first major land acquisition. The Masiker Store was eventually located on part of that Kelley land purchase. The Masiker's Kelley purchase came down Bear Lake Road toward Route 380 and Stockton but stopped where Harriet Campbell currently lives.

According to Emery R, *"it came past the creek, but not very far, and included the strip down Muskie Point Road. The Campbells wanted to make some use of their land but didn't want to build a road. So, Emery A made a deal with them that if they'd sell him a fifty foot access, he'd build the road down to the lake. And they'd have right of way. That was the only piece added later to the original Kelley purchase."*

The land where the store was later built

Emery A later built the first house going up Bacheller Hill Road from the four corners for his sister, Margie, who lived in West Virginia but spent summers at Bear Lake. It later became and remains the Orloff house.

Claiming the Swamp and Channeling the Creek: In his interview, the late Marshall Kelly described how he helped Emery A clear the swamp when he came back from the war. Emery R, however, disputed it saying that although he was down there during the creek clearout, Marshall was only about ten years old then. According to Emery R *"The creek used to* *come down under Bear Lake Road and then spread out all over the place; there was no defined creek bed. So, that's where part of the dynamiting came in, blasting stumps to get them out of the way to make the creek run straight, and then again with the slip scrapper, which is a big scoop shovel with two handles on it. You hook it to a tractor or horses, and you follow this thing and hang on to the handles for dear life. If it hits a stump or root, it would catch and throw you up in the air because when you got it full, you pushed the handles down and it would just skid along the ground until you got it to where you wanted to dump the load, and then grab the handles and turn them down; and it would dig in and flip it upside down and dump the dirt out. Then you'd go and get another scoop of dirt. That's how they did it."*

"Once they got the channel of the creek open, it flowed within the channel. But until then, it was mostly swamp, and cows would get stuck in it." Emery R remembered going down there to free up a cow with block and tackles from out of the mud holes. *"It dried up fairly well once the creek was channeled. Mostly what was left was brush. It was a tangle, a jungle. We'd cut all of it down that we could; then burn it. We'd take the larger poles home after getting the brush off of them, and burn them for fire wood because we heated our houses with wood stoves. That old cook stove ate up a lot of wood. We spent a lot of hours clearing brush and taking down trees for firewood clearing out that swamp,"* he said.

Land and brush clearing

Land and brush clearing

Building the Canals: The canals were dug before construction on the Masiker Store began. *"The first canal was dug pretty much by hand with a slip scrapper behind those old whoopy tractors* [i.e., handmade tractors]. *Then we dynamited; in those days you could buy dynamite. One day when they were dyna-miting tree stumps, I got hit in the head by a piece of stump because we used electric caps; and apparently we didn't have* *enough wire and couldn't get far enough away from the blast. We used the battery on the tractor to get the electric charge to set the dynamite off, and then we'd hide under the tractor.*

We started the first canal by hand; then we got somebody in there with a drag line and enlarged it some more. The second one wasn't dug until I came back here from Connecticut [in the mid 60's]; and I bought a back hoe and went to digging on that one. Then we got someone else to come in and enlarge it; then you could get a big machine in there on solid ground. We didn't have machines like we do now to do that work."

Store in winter before the Workshop was built

Handmade "Whoopy" tractor

Building the Store: Emery R, his dad and his brother Bob started making brick materials for the store a year or two before they actually started construction on the store. Store construction began in about 1962, after Emery R had gone to work in Connecticut, but before the "shop," the building to the left of the store, was built. *"We started making the bricks for the store in the basement and the garage of the place up the road* [the Kelly farm house]. *We made some forms, and we poured four 8"X16" bricks. Then Dad made a guillotine thing, a jack that would cut the bricks and the edges made from the blades of snowplows. When the bricks had dried a certain amount, he would slide the brick into this thing, work the jack, and bang he'd cut them. That's why when you look at those bricks you'll see they all have rough surfaces. They'd be big bricks and we'd cut them in half and make two bricks out of one. And he got some dye from somewhere which we'd put into the* [concrete] *mix, black colored streaks in them, some red in them. We spent hours and hours making bricks. When you're using a little cement mixer in the garage, making bricks and cutting* them, your hands had blisters on them from handling the rough edges. They're concrete and that took a year or two.

The ground where the store is was three feet higher than it is now. There was a big rounded knoll there. They dug it all out and used it for fill down lower. That's why there's a flat spot there now; there wasn't a flat spot there before. And where those cottages are along the canal, it was very wet. You came off the road and you dropped down quite a steep embankment. The store is on original ground, but the rest of the cottages along the canal are on four or more feet of fill. The other parts we filled with stuff that came out of the canals."

Emery A and Velma

Aerial view photo taken by Tommy Harris

Emery A and Velma eventually moved from the farm to the store. As Emery R describes it, *"He built his own home made saw mill. Those rafters in the store; they're all from his saw mill which was next to that original building, the ones in the basement too. We got the poles from the twelve to fifteen acre piece of property across from the Basket Factory. Poles are beams/ rafters/etc. I don't know that they had a name for the store. Dad didn't worry that much about naming things. My cousin took some aerial shots about then."*

"Mother sold the store to Richard and Kay Orloff on May 22, 1979. Orloff then sold it to Art and Marlene Clever on May 15, 1981, but Mother still had the mortgage on it. I still hang onto the Conservation Club land that comes up next to Clever; the trees are mostly mine except those near Emery [M].

Emery R left high school in 1959, but since there were no jobs around, he went to Connecticut, where his aunt and uncle lived, following his brother Bob who had taken a job at Kamen

Aircraft in Windsor Locks, Connecticut. *"They said that if I'd come out there, I certainly would find a job in Hartford, actually East Hartford, working for Pratt and Whitney.* [That was] *a year or so after I got out of school, but I had to wait until I was 18 to get a job. That was 1961-62."*

Recollections of his father, Emery A: *"My dad made arrow heads that no one can tell if they were original or not. We used to age them. He cut gem stones, and had a tumbler. He'd make the arrow head and put it in the tumbler and age it a couple of hundred years. You couldn't tell the difference. Mother had a collection of arrow heads in the store, mixed together, and I cannot tell the difference. He found a couple out here in back of my place. It wasn't a typical shape, it was a little different. He never hired anything done. Anything we needed done, he'd figure out how to do something. I questioned that practice, spending x number of hours doing something that could have been done quicker and easier another way. But how do you fault someone who succeeded? Never owed anyone a dime. Never took anything from anybody, and always treated people right, as far as I know."*

Asked who bought the former Y property on his side of Bear Lake along Route 380, Emery R answered that *"Beardsley bought it from Clifford Pierce; and Walter Hornburg bought it from Beardsley. The County shut the Y Camp down; then Pierce* [who still owned that piece] *sold that piece of property to Walt Hornburg. Hornburg's family used to own where Leroy Pierce once was. Beardsley sold Hornburg anything that couldn't be farmed. There are high spots and knolls in the swamp. I can go onto it* [from his land]*; but Hornburg had to go through a ¼ mile of swamp to get to his high ground."* [The Hornburg property was bought by Dennis Sabella in 2014.]

Recollections of the Le Roy Pierce Property: *"I remember the old ice house behind Leroy Pierce's large house on Bear*

83

Lake Road [where the Pierce/Alden/Bob Dobbins house is now]. *It was once a hotel, I think. That was all shut down when we came here. Pierce and his wife Minnie had one boy, Howard. Never knew the woman who lived there after Minnie died. Her name was Maude Shoemaker. 'Maude and her cats.' My Dad built a house,* (now the Dottie McQuiggan house) *for Maude when Roy died. Roy's land went from the east side of Gilbert Drive to where Maude's house was, where it joined Kelley/Masiker land to the corner."*

Remembering the basket factory, Emery R explained *"the Snell family started that Basket Factory. Originally it started out as a grape basket factory. A lot of people in the area were involved in making fruit baskets."* Emery R remembers going up and down the roads selling the fruit baskets. *"There were packing houses down there in Brocton, with horses and wagons waiting to load baskets into the trains. There were stickers that farmers put on their baskets.* [Some baskets were not made in the basket factories] *The Kashbohms, who had a lot of stuff in their garage, had their own set up for making their own baskets. They bought their veneer from somewhere else. Farmers made baskets during the winter."*

Emery R also Remembered Clifford Case: *"He was an entrepreneur; he set up this ice cream stand on the* [Bear Lake] *Corners and had a couple of ice cream machines and made ice cream sandwiches. He'd load them in the back of his pickup truck and sell them door to door. Then he decided he wanted to have a stand on the corner and had my Dad build it for him. It was an ice cream and hot dog stand. Clifford was a kind of go getter, always had some bright idea. He was married to Dan O'Brien's and Dottie O'Brien McQuiggan's mother, Dorothy. About that same time, Mother and Dad decided to build their store."*

Emery R's brother, Bob, currently lives in West Palm Beach, Florida. Their mother Velma lived there too until she died in Florida in 1985, and her ashes were brought to Bear Lake. Emery A died in 1976. Their sister, Margie lives in Ocala, Florida. Bob's daughter, Kate, married to David Snell, currently lives up on Kelly Hill Road.

Like his father, Emery R and his son Emery M are known at Bear Lake for being able to do anything that you need done. Many Bear Lake residents have had septic systems, walls, parking ramps and driveways done by them. Emery R and his family still live on Route 380 on the south side of the lake from the larger lake community on Bear Lake Road; but they are in the process of moving to Kentucky and spend more time there each year. He has already built a house and barn there. The entrepreneurial, Emery R Masiker family has been and continues to be an important resource to the Bear Lake community and will be missed if/when they move away. His son, Emery M, referred to as "Young" or "Junior," continues to live on Bear Lake Road, where he operates a tree farm. In 2016 he bought back the property once owned by his grandparents and has improved it considerably since then to the delight of his Bear Lake neighbors.

The three Emerys and their families have been and still are important to the history of Bear Lake.

CHAPTER 11
THE CLIFFORD
PIERCE FAMILIES

T he Clifford Pierce family, like the Luther Leroy Pierce family, although not related to each other, had a strong influence on Bear Lake. The Clifford Pierce family is introduced in this chapter, and the Luther LeRoy Pierce family in the next chapter.

Clifford Pierce married Ruth Lazell in Stockton in 1907. He later established a family campground, "Pierce Acres," on what was called Gravel Point on the south side of Bear Lake. Next to that family campground in 1928, he established a YMCA/YWCA camp, known as the Camp-in-the-Woods or the "Y" Camp. He gave it free to the Chautauqua County YMCA organization. This non-profit, non-denominational Camp continued until the County Health Department forced its closing in 1975. [The Y Camp is discussed in more detail in Chapter 19.]

The Y Camp and the Pierce family campground covered about a third of the nine hundred plus acre Pierce property that formed Pierce Acres. Most of the rest of the acreage, on the south side of Route 380 and along Bowen Road, comprised the two hundred Jersey cow Pierce dairy farm, managed by Max Pierce, Clifford's brother. The campground was colorfully described by several of Clifford Pierce's grandchildren, who either lived there during the summer or, when old enough, attended Camp-in-the-Woods next door. One of those grandchildren, Ruth Szumigala, who lives on Bear Lake, described *"the two-room cottage/cabin with no water, electricity, or indoor plumbing."* Her father, Richard Wang (married to Rachel Pierce one of

Clifford's and Ruth's four children) *"put bunk beds in the room in the back; there was a little room, which served as a kitchen, and a front room that had a table and chairs and beds. The cabin was close to the lake and to a sandbox with steps leading down to the lakefront."*

Pierce children & friends in the sandbox

Pierce Family: Clifford Pierce with in back row Ruth, Westrum and in front row Richard, John, and Betty

The Y Camp buildings were located to the left of the Pierce cabin; and at some point, Clifford's son, John "Jack" Pierce, built a separate cabin for his family about one hundred feet from the main Clifford Pierce cabin. When Camp began each summer, it became the "Admiral's Cabin" for the Y Camp director.

John Pierce's cabin

Grandson John Pierce ("Jack" Pierce's son) remembers that the Clifford Pierce cabin had a porch, there was a dock for boats, and his mother and father water skied on the lake.

Rachel Pierce, one of Clifford and Ruth Lazell Pierce's four children, wrote a *"Recollection"* in the Town of Stockton *"Old Fashioned Days"* pamphlet for September 12 and 13, 1992, p.57. It reads: *"Gravel Point: How I loved that place, every rut in the old road leading to it. There was a gate that separated the pasture from the woods and John* [her brother] *always made the one sitting in the front seat of the car get out and open it. One time it happened to be Grandma Lazell ... and I remember her climbing out and trying to unlatch the heavy gate. She did it!*

I can hear the frogs, buried in the lily pads and croaking away; the light bumping of the boats as they gently hit the docks; the smell of Viola's (Cumming's) ginger cookies (from the camp kitchen); the huge camp fire and the songs we sang as we watched the logs blaze away; the hissing sound of the Coleman lantern as I wrote for my Master's Degree."

More of the Pierce family background is included in the chapter *"Family of Clifford Pierce"* by another granddaughter Martha (Patty) Fellows Petsch, daughter of Marion [Pierce] and Lloyd Fellows) in *the Septquicentennial Memory Book, 1821-1996, The Township of Stockton, New York, 1996*, compiled by Helen Piersons, Town of Stockton Historian. Piersons tells us that Clifford Pierce's grandparents were Christopher Columbus Pierce and Salina Todd Pierce, and his parents were Luman Pierce and Clara Derby Pierce. Luman Pierce was an agent with the Empire State Degree of Honor (an insurance company which was started in Stockton). Born in 1882, at age 19 Clifford began his long career with the YMCA by becoming Assistant Secretary of the YMCA in Washington, D.C. In 1906 he was appointed General Secretary of the Army YMCA at Fort Monroe, Virginia; and in 1907, he returned to Stockton, as was said above, to marry Ruth Lazell, a member of a prominent family in Stockton where her father, Lavern W. Lazell operated a private bank.

Later, Clifford went with his wife to Fort Leavenworth, Kansas to establish a YMCA there, and by 1909, had become General Secretary of the YMCA of Wichita, Kansas, and later was Secretary of the Kansas State YMCA. Clifford and Ruth returned to Stockton in 1920 where he purchased the three hundred acres that included the Pierce's Y Camp. Clifford became Vice President in the Pierce & Hedrick fundraising company with his uncle Lyman Pierce and Bayard M. Hedrick, the Vice President and General Manager. Pierce & Hedrick had offices in New York City, San Francisco, and Stockton, New York [Yes! an office in little Stockton].

Clifford later became a "gentleman farmer" and the President of the Stockton Town Picnic for twenty years, from 1923–25, 1927–1930, and 1932–1944. He was Director of the Chautauqua County Fair and was a prominent member of various clubs and organizations. During this time, he continued as director of financial campaigns for philanthropic and religious organizations, and according to his obituary *(The Post Journal,* Monday, October 30, 1960) *"millions of dollars were collected under* [his] *direction over the years. He directed the organization and publicity for several of the early community chest drives in Jamestown."* In short, Clifford was a very prominent community leader while living on Bear Lake and in Stockton.

Clifford and Ruth Pierce had five children: Robert (who died young) Marion (who married Lloyd Fellows and had two children), John (who married Emmy Connell and had one child), Rachel (who married Richard Wang and had three children), and Martha (who married Tom Zoller and had four children). Ruth Wang Szumigala (daughter of Rachel and Richard Wang and a current Bear Lake resident) grew up in Stockton. Her family lived in the tenant house on her Pierce grandparents' dairy farm, where her father worked for Clifford and Max Pierce. The Wang family eventually moved into the Pierce house on Bowen Road after her grandmother, Ruth, died in 1950. Ruth attended elementary school in Stockton, where her

mother taught elementary grades and music, and then went on to Cassadaga Valley Central School.

Ruth and her husband Ed Szumigala bought their Bear Lake cottage on the opposite side of the lake from her grandparents' land from Dave Hoestler of Angola about fifteen years ago, and it has become a regular gathering place during the summer for her family and cousins. The Szumigalas also bought Helen and Don Piersons' cottage next door, which they later sold to Judy McQueary's son Mike and his family, its current residents.

Pierce Family: front row--Clifford, Ruth, John; back row—Rachel, Martha, Emmy

Ruth confirmed, what others had said, that the Clifford Pierce family was not related to the Roy and Minnie Pierce on north side of the lake. She agreed, however, that the Clifford Pierces were related to the Crockers (see the Crocker Chapter 5). As told in the Crocker chapter, Elizabeth Crocker, longtime County Historian and her mother, Ella, stayed in a cottage on the Pierce family campground before moving to the north side of the lake. That cottage that they stayed in had been the ice house at the Brocton railroad station, then was moved first to Pierce Acres, and later moved across the lake to become the boat livery for Walt Lamkin's store, and finally became the Johnston's cottage, which it remains today!

Before Clifford Pierce died in 1960, he had sold his farm and all the rest of his other property, including the Pierce family campground and the Y Camp to John Beardsley (in 1953). *"Clifford wanted the Y Camp to stay a camp, but Beardsley didn't want that,"* Helen Piersons said. So Clifford retained it until he eventually sold it to John Beardsley in 1969. Six years later in 1975, the County Health Department shut the Y Camp down because the area would not "perk" sufficiently to put in a large enough septic system to accommodate the increasing number of campers. Subsequently in 1979, Beardsley sold the Camp property to Walter Hornburg and the rest of the original lakeside Pierce acreage to Emery R Masiker. Hornburg built a house and put a dock out, but his family never took to it, so the house and dock were soon removed. Hornburg was connected to the Roy Pierce family on the north side of Bear Lake. His heirs eventually sold the three hundred plus acres to Dennis Sabella a lumber manufacturer from Tidioute, PA in 2014. When concern about the development of the land affecting the bio control weed program at Bear Lake was brought to his attention, Sabella promised to not do anything with the land *"for at least twenty years."*

The Clifford and Ruth Pierce family of ten grandchildren and many cousins stay in contact with each other, many of them visiting the Szumigala's Bear Lake cottage each summer. Ruth is the only one of them who still owns a cottage on Bear Lake, where she is seen most days out on her front porch or on the lake in her kayak. The Pierce extended family has enriched the Bear Lake community for decades.

CHAPTER 12
LUTHER LEROY PIERCE FAMILY

A s noted in earlier chapters, everyone we interviewed mentioned the Luther Leroy Pierce family. They were among the most important families here from the turn of the twentieth century to the 1950s. Although none of Pierce descendants still live in the Bear Lake community, we were fortunate to find detailed information about them. The Blodgett-Pierce Family Website, maintained by Steven Vannier, provided extensive information and pictures of the Pierces and Blodgetts. Vannier is one of the family historians as well as web-master for that web-site, and shares historian duties with Douglas Nelson. Minnie Blodgett was Roy Pierce's wife, and several Blodgetts and a Pierce grandson were all interviewed at several Pierce-Landas and Blodgett reunions in Stockton. Additional anecdotal recollections from the Bogner, O'Brien and McQuiggan families (in Chapter 4), from the Rawson and Dobbins families (in Chapter 6) and from the Clifford Pierce families (in Chapter 11) enriched this Pierce history.

Maude Reynolds from the
Blodgett-Pierce website

We learned that Luther Leroy Pierce, known as Roy or Leroy, born August 13, 1870, was one of ten children of Enos Allen Pierce and Julia Evalina (Landas) Pierce. Roy's first marriage was to Maude Reynolds who died soon after. He married Minnie Mabel Lucretia Blodgett (born June 13, 1876, the daughter of Milo and Aurelia [Russ] Blodgett) on February 8, 1899. They had seven children, only two of whom survived infancy: Luther Leroy (Roy) Jr, born July 7, 1899, and a second son, Howard Wilson Pierce born August 12, 1913.

Luther Leroy and Minnie Pierce in the 1890s. Luther is wearing his fireman's uniform from the Fredonia Volunteer Fenner Hose Company

The Luther LeRoy Pierce farm comprised all of that property along the middle of Bear Lake Road and up the hill toward Kelly Hill Road from the George Cooper farm's line on the west side of Gilbert Drive to the western edge of the Kelley farm on Bear Lake Road, around one hundred eighty-five acres. In August of 1921, Roy decided to separate his land into parcels, and had surveyor C. Burton lay out twenty-eight lots, each fifty feet by one hundred fifty feet, called "Allotment A," for the land west of his house. In 1925, he had Burton lay out sixteen additional lots, fifty feet by one hundred feet, called "Allotment B," behind the 1921 surveyed lots. And, finally in

July 1941, he had surveyor James P. Morrissey lay out forty-five lots, labelled A through E, each lot fifty feet by one hundred feet called "Allotment C," to the east of his house. He sold lots on either side of his own lakeside lot which had four hundred forty-one feet of lake frontage along Bear Lake Road. According to his descendants, Pierce probably chose Bear Lake for his farm because *"the land was cheap, was relatively cleared, was easy to farm, and was isolated"*.

The Pierce farmhouse, an impressive two-story, ten bedroom house with a cupola, was listed in local advertisements as the "Bear Lake House." Behind it to the north was an ice house, and to the east a milk house which was "cooled" by piping that ran to one of the springs behind what is currently the Frasier/Lanni/Fox/ Martz house. Next to the milk house was a barn for his cows, and next to it, but closer to the road, an orchard where picnics were held. Pierce also sold vanilla ice cream from a roadside stand on Bear Lake Road to those picnicking.

The Pierce Farmhouse/Hotel

Rear View of Pierce Farmhouse showing
from left to right, the ice cream stand, the
milk house, farmhouse, and the barn

95

There was also a boat livery on the Pierce lakefront. Dorothy Dobbins, who currently lives nextdoor to the former Pierce house, described the boats as *"metal with a rounded keel (rather than the usual flat keel)."* She also tells of a tragedy on the lake. *"One day a young couple rented a boat with their young baby. Somehow the baby fell overboard on the far side of the lake. The father jumped in to save the baby, and the father and baby were never seen again. The boats were not very stable and wobbled when you got into them."*

Advertisements in the 1936 and 1938 souvenir program of the Annual Stockton Town Picnic listed: "L.L. Pierce, Proprietor/Bear Lake House" and a "Bear Lake House, L.L.Pierce Proprietor." The latter ad included *"On Sundays a chicken dinner for $1.00 on order was featured, as well as board and lodging at $2.00 per day and up, and homemade ice cream daily." "Boating and fishing"* and *"rest and recreation"* were also advertised. People would *"sit in the dining or the living room or in the picnic area to eat these chicken dinners."* In the 1938 and repeated in the 1939 Town Picnic programs, the advertisements read: *"L.L.Pierce/BEAR LAKE/Boat Livery- Free Picnic Grounds/Ice Cream/Lots for Sale/ Phone 1352 Brocton/ P.O. Stockton, N.Y."* The 1939 ad validates Dobbin's recollection about Pierce's boat livery, that others did not recall, but remember Walter Lamkin's boat livery at the other end of the Lake (currently the Johnston cottage).

According to Judy McQueary, the Pierce farmhouse had *"ten bedrooms with feather-tick mattresses, a living room as well as a parlor, a large kitchen, a study and an additional bedroom on the first floor."* At one point in its history, it served as a hostel, and at another, it housed New York City children under a "Sunshine Kids" program. Mr. Pierce would *"let the neighborhood children go up into the cupola, as long as they had their mothers' permission."* It also had bats, which local boys like her cousin, Tom O'Brien (interviewed in Chapter 4), were hired to kill. For a long time, Pierce was the only one at Bear Lake to have a telephone, #1352.

At a Pierce-Blodgett reunion, Linda Blodgett (daughter of Julia and Boyd Blodgett and grand-niece of Leroy) talked about visiting the Pierce house: "*As a little girl, I visited him* [Uncle Roy] *on a regular basis, when he lived in a big house that is no longer there. We had picnics there, and the Pierce reunions started there.*" The Blodgett-Pierce family history notes that the first Pierce family reunion was held in 1885. Pictures showing reunions at the Pierce farm are available on the family website. If you go to the 1937 reunion photograph, each of the one hundred people in the photo will be identified for you when you put the cursor on them.

Pierce Reunion of 1937

Linda contined : "*my mother and dad visited every summer because LeRoy was my father's uncle. This would be in the 1950s. My three sisters and I learned to fish with bamboo poles on Uncle Roy's property there, but I don't know what he did for a living.*" Marilyn Tastor, related to the Pierce-Blodgett family on her mother's side, attended reunions there from the time she was three years old until her Uncle Roy died in 1958. Linda said that she went more frequently and remembers her mother warning her: "*Now, don't touch anything. And all those cats. And no, we're not going to the bathroom here! It was a hostel at one time. City kids from New York City came for four or five years in the summer. Maybe dad and mom helped to support that venture. I don't remember that. After Minnie died* [in 1934], *the reunion carried on with the chicken and biscuits tradition."*

At another Pierce-Blodgett Reunion, Leroy Pierce, Jr.'s son, William (Bill) and his sister Katy Putnam told us that the Pierce *"front porch fell off one year, and there was a big porte-cochere along the east side. Leroy [Sr.] was about 5'8-5'9; and sat in the window and watched what went down the road. We would come to his house from Cortland, New York where I grew up. Many reunions were held at his house. I don't remember Minnie because I was born in 1936. Grandfather didn't remarry. I do remember Maude Shoemaker, grandfather's housekeeper.*

My folks remember folks riding in on their bicycles. The bedroom furniture was still there. Bunk beds, the big center room had four bunk beds. The front room had a regular bed in it, and the room in back had bunk beds. Uncle Howard's room [Leroy Pierce Sr.'s other son] *was up there in the cupola. My dad went to Fredonia High School, and my mother* [Olive Schoonhoven] *grew up in Versailles, New York, which is where my folks were buried."*

Katy added that her grandfather. *". . . had dairy cows, but just for their own use, not a huge herd. He had an electric five horse motor that was three inches in diameter with which he would chop the ice and store it in sawdust in the barn. He made ice cream, and I licked off the beaters, and he had a milk house cooled by a spring. He had a 'ram' up on the hill which was an hydraulic device. If you had a lot of water, the ram compressed the air on the top and forced the water down the pipe and also up to the second floor of the house. Plus they had another pipe that ran all the time in the back shed and that gave water. The milk house also ran off that spring. When I was here about ten years ago, I stopped and went up to the spring, and there was a keg of beer getting cold."*

Asked how often she stayed at Pierce's, Katy answered: *"Maybe a week or two in the summer and sometimes for*

Christmas or Thanksgiving or a weekend. I wasn't around then, but my folks told me that one time they couldn't get up the hill because the Ford ran out of fuel. Up the driveway, the same old maples are still there. My dad went to Hamilton College and graduated in 1921. Uncle Howard went to Cornell and graduated in three years. Howard was a chemist. He would also come back and stay between semesters."

Bill Putnam's father, LeRoy Jr, lived in Cortland and was a math teacher and baseball coach. His mother went to Syracuse University and was a teacher until she went to work for D.C.Heath publisher. Bill, like his Dad, went to Hamilton and then Syracuse in civil engineering. He also went to Thailand to teach people there how to set up a water system, and later worked for the City of Syracuse as Commissioner of Public Works. His wife was a teacher for 30 years.

Bill saw Leroy Pierce for the last time in 1957. *"He died in 1958 at the age of eighty-eight. He had lived for so many years selling property and running his small farm. Emmett Kelly was one of my uncle's close friends. I didn't know Marshall Kelly, but I remember Bill Snell was up on the hill."*

In addition to his descendants' recollections, LeRoy Pierce is mentioned in the *Farm Directory and Reference Book Chautauqua County, New York*. (New York: American Agriculturalist, Orange Judd Publishers, 1918, 169) as follows: *"Pierce, L.L. (Minnie B.) 2ch[children] 'Bear Lake Farm' farmer (hay, grain) O[wns] 88 a[cres—farm rent only acres] rd [rural delivery] # 28 [route number] Stockton Pomfret tn [township] T[elephone]H[highway] 94."* He is also mentioned in Cathryn Berndt's *Stockton: Seen Through the Rear View Mirror.* (1987): (p.70) *"Leroy Pierce purchased the Methodist Episcopal church building in 1941. The building was torn down in 1942 by Manley and Donald Piersons. Some of the lumber was used to build a barn on Pierce's farm at Bear Lake; (p. 74) Leroy Pierce was a member of a Committee of Five (chaired by Clifford Pierce) to consider federation of the Stockton Baptist Church and the*

Methodist Episcopal Church in 1929. The Committee drafted Articles of Federation in 1930. Leroy Pierce was elected to a three year term on the Federated Council; (p. 97) Leroy Pierce was a Trustee of Warren District #6 School. Maps of 1854 and 1867 show descendants of Calvin Warren settled on Lots 47 and 48. And Ray Kelley was also a Trustee of the same school."

In 1949 Leroy Pierce was also one of the incorporators when the Bear Lake Property Owners Association was formed in response to Brocton's taking more than the legal amount of water from Bear Lake to fill their low water reservoir. After Minnie Pierce died on May 17, 1934, Maude Shoemaker became house-keeper to Pierce and brought her daughters Phyllis and Judy with her to live in his house.

According to Dorothy Dobbins, *"When Mr. Pierce died in 1958, James Rawson* [her father] *had already introduced his sister, Elsie, to Everett Robert (John) Alden, who was a very successful lawyer from Rahway, New Jersey and worked at Socony-Mobil. Mr. Everett Alden bought the Pierce estate; and James Rawson helped dismantle the Pierce farmhouse and used timbers from it to build the Alden house in 1960 where Everett and his second wife Elsie lived."*

Leroy Pierce was a descendent of Ichabod Pierce who moved his family from Vermont to Chautauqua County in 1820. Clearly one of the most prominent residents on Bear Lake, he remains a Bear Lake legend to this day. http://blodgett-pierce.org

CHAPTER 13
THE PIERSONS FAMILY

H elen Piersons, Town of Stockton Historian, provided us
with much interesting historical and anecdotal information about living on Bear Lake, and several important maps.
As the catalyst for writing *A History of Bear Lake* specifically
through the stories of longtime lakeside residents, we are in
her debt.

The Piersons arrived at Bear Lake in the 1940s. According
to Helen, *"It was in the late 1940s. We bought a cottage up
there. We enjoyed it for about 50 years and sold it about four
years ago to the Szumigalas. The cottage we had is now the
McQueary's cottage, and we bought the lot next to us (now
Szumigala's). We were the Piersons who operated and owned
Stockton Sales with Leonard Deering in 1966 and afterwards.*

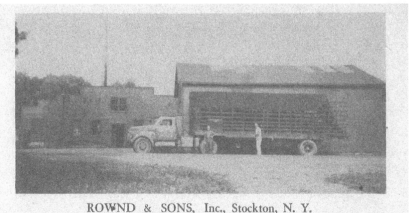

ROWND & SONS, Inc., Stockton, N. Y.

Stockton Sales

We also owned the lot on the lakefront across from our cottage where we dug out a channel to put our boats in. Elton Hall had the house beside our lot and a family named Hoestlers was next. Farther to the right of our cottage [going west] was the Fuller and then the Frasier and then the Bogner cottages We had two large willow trees in front of our cottage that we had to cut down.

We lived in Stockton after getting married in 1941 and moved here [to Railroad Avenue] *in 1943 where we continue to live. Our seventy-fifth anniversary was December 3, 2016. A lot of people have come into our lives, and we've enjoyed them all. I've always been a people person all my life."*

In our September 2009 interview, Helen described the Bear Lake Cribbage group: *"My husband played; he still does at 93; tonight he's over to Mayville to play cribbage. I never played too much. I always thought he had a better time when I didn't, if you know what I mean. I never could count as fast as he could. Maybe I'll stay out of that."*

Describing their land on Bear Lake, Helen said that *"the first thing that comes to mind is that in back of us had been pasture, and there were little seedlings coming up. Now, of course, it's all trees. Somewhere there is a picture of that hillside. But that was amazing how that filled in.*

Hillside above the Piersons' cottage

102

There was a spring back in there that served about three houses. However, when we moved there we had a well. We used the spring for washing and baths. It wasn't our cup of tea to drink from the spring. And the spring was there until the State went up there and found that they were not satisfactory to the health code. They tested them and the people who owned the property weren't doing anything about the water. In fact, it was in our deeds that that spring water was always to be supplied. They refused to do anything to bring the springs up to the health code; so everyone got their wells dug. This was in the 1960s. It was after the big Pierce house was torn down and the Alden house was built.

We never did much fishing but we did catch a muskie at the beginning. Before he went into Stockton Sales, Don had a cattle business, and we didn't have time. [Don also operated a trucking company.]

DONALD PIERSON, Stockton, N. Y.
Trucking and Hauling - Phone 64F2

Don Piersons' trucking company advertisement in the Stockton Town Picnic brochure for 1956

I was secretary to the basket factory (the one where Stockton Sales was later located) owned by Thompson Rownd, and worked there about 25 years. I started there as a secretary and worked my way up to a Manager's position; but the biggest part of our business went South. Mr. Rownd felt it was better there to get raw material; big logs were getting harder and harder to get. He went out and got timber, veneered it to make the baskets. We made some grape baskets but mostly tomato baskets. We shipped many railroad cars of what we called "splint" baskets like the 8 or 12 quart baskets to the New England states, Massachusetts. Then in the winter we had a big business in making the mushroom baskets which we shipped to Kennett Square Pennsylvania. Kennett Square was a big grower at that time. They would take carloads of baskets".

I did quite a bit of traveling 1978-9 throughout New York State for the Rebekah organization, and I'd be in the eastern part of the state and people would ask 'what's new at Stockton Sales?' There was a fellow in Saugerties who collected a lot of coins, and Don has collected a lot of coins over the years, and they became quite good friends and did a lot of business."

Discussing our book, Helen suggested that *"it cannot be organized in terms of businesses, schools, mayors, etc. Although there was a school at Kelly's Corners; there were very few families and very early it was mostly farm land. For that area, the oral interview is your best bet. Organize it around families and who owned which cottages when. Bring it down to date. The history of your home is in your title and your deed."* [We followed Helen's suggestions for organizing this book and also for using our Title Search document to trace our cottage's history in Chapter 15.]

Asked about the Masiker family, another prominent family on Bear Lake, Helen offered: *"I think that that family is one of the families that my husband moved down here from Pittsburgh. There was another family that he moved from Pittsburg into Stockton, but not to work in the basket factory. Velma Masiker's husband built the store using trees that he had cut from that area. He did watch repair on the side; he was a jack of all trades."*

Like most other Bear Lake residents, Helen remembers the Pierce house as a very interesting one. *"People from around the country would bicycle there. It was a hostel at one time. Pierce sold ice cream and there was a picnic ground. Going east from Pierce's farm were: Hoch, Berndt, O'Brien, an Italian couple* [Fennos], *Californians* [Greens], *Tabasco, Case , Bogner, Frasier, Fuller, Szumigala, Pierson, vacant lot, then Dana Riforgiato (who lived in Fredonia), Dottie McQuiggan, another house* [now Fiegl] *then the corner house* (McQuiggan) *and O'Brien on the opposite side of Kelly Hill Road"*.

In 1954, a plan was introduced to flood Bear Lake valley. Helen recalls that *"The 1954 planned flooding was such a crazy thing; and the Town of Stockton got up in arms about it."* [It never happened.] She also remembers the Sahle picnic grove [now George Clever's house.] *"I almost think it was up on that side road, Lawrence Road. One time when we were up there, someone got to talking about eventually putting a road in the back of our cottage. They wouldn't have lakefront but lake view.* [Pierce did survey his land to create a road and building lots.]

Helen and Don enjoyed their cottage. *"We used to move up there Memorial Day; then we'd move back on Labor Day. Later we stayed until the beginning of October. When we were both working, we tended to use it for weekends only. Then, when we retired, we'd spend six months up there and six months down here. People would say 'but you live so close'; but it is relaxing up there. That's the part that I miss the most. Just sitting and watching the lake. We sold because it got to be too much for my husband with all the lawns to mow, and we have two different apartment buildings here in Stockton to take care of. We decided that we could get along without it. We drove up there the other day. He doesn't drive that much anymore. He said let's drive up and see what they've done to the cottage. Well they've extended the cottage. It looks great. I'm so glad someone is taking care of it."* [Mike McQueary, Judy McQueary's son and his family live in it now.]

"*Judy McQueary and Ruth Szumigala were good friends. Judy would bring her two granddaughters to visit our kittens.*" About those kittens, she once had a surprise: " *we had left our cats in Stockton. I was away on a trip, and Fluffy came all the way down here* [from Stockton to Bear Lake] *for something to eat. The next day I showed her the comb, and she came and started purring. She later had her litter up in the woods. We tried to find them, but we never could, until she eventually brought them down to our porch, five black and white kittens. She brought them down when she was ready. How she found her way from Stockton to Bear Lake is still a mystery. Wild. And we fussed with them and got them domesticated on the front porch. And before we left there we had them all given away. She had about three litters a year; and the last year she wore herself out; and we had to have her put down. We had two cats for nine years until a friend died who had a cat, and we then had three cats.*"

Described as a "great lady" by Bear Lake residents, Stockton Historian, Helen Piersons still lives on Route 58 on the hill going to Cassadaga. She and her *Septquicentennial Memory Book, 1821-1996,* about the Township of Stockton were helpful in writing this book.

CHAPTER 14
THE WISER FAMILY

The Wiser family was at Bear Lake as early as the 1940s. A summer resident once again, Martha Wiser's recollections detail what life on the lake was like back then. *"I have a feeling my father fished here in the late 1940s early 50s. I do remember that we were here when I was in grade school which would have been between 1950 and 1955. We just had the land, for a picnic area (where the late Arden & Anne Berndt home is today).* [Martha's parents Harold P. Wiser and Barbara L. Wiser bought Lot 1-E from Roy Pierce in 1954]. *"We had a dock and a boat. Then in 1955, when we were getting ready to move to Buffalo because my father's job was going to take him there, I remember having a cottage* [at Bear Lake] *because our house in Buffalo was not built yet. So we lived in that cottage from the time we sold our house in Dunkirk—about six months. The cottage was pretty much finished; the plumbing was in; I remember the septic system being a big deal for my father and uncle and how to rig that. Our cottage in 1954 and 1955 was just a square with partitioned rooms, where you could see over the top. There were three bedrooms with curtains on the doors. The front of the cottage had a kitchen and a dining room overlooking the lake.*

One morning I got up and went into the kitchen to have breakfast, and I looked at the lake (it must have been September or October), and the lake was totally covered in white. It snowed last night? My mother and father said 'look carefully.' It was covered with snow geese. That was in 1955. I don't know whether they were ever there again.

Our property went way up the hill to the top. We used to climb up there, but I don't know how far it went. There was an empty lot (on the west side) that didn't belong to us. . . I'm not sure we owned up the hill. Berndts bought the cottage about 1956 or so, and they may have incorporated the cottage into the back of their house." [Arden Berndt later bought that empty lot from Luther LeRoy Pierce and the lots behind the house from Bob Dobbins.] *"I remember coming out of the front door of our cottage to visit Millie Ebeling. I went over there for breakfast. Ebeling's cottage is now Tom and Marce O'Brien's.*

We lived in Dunkirk until my freshman year of high school in 1954 and came to Bear Lake quite often. My father had trouble getting us to come here when my brothers and I got really busy with things in school. He said he'd sell it and eventually did.

I remember Bear Lake Property Owners Association picnics; there were quite a few people there in those days. I also remember that almost every cottage had a raft, because it wasn't fun putting your feet down in the muck. I always wore water shoes. You swam from your dock out to the raft. It was a quick drop off where we lived. I went to the Y Camp two years in a row. I can remember bringing boats and canoes over to the store that Lamkin had then." [Lamkin's store was located on what was then called "Cub Cove." That store/house recently sold; the Martzes have moved down the lake to the former Lanni/Fox house, and Lanni/Fox moved down the other direction to the former Cooper/Lamkin/Dorset/Frame house]

"We had a row boat; and we'd take it out a ways, and it filled with water; and Dad would bring it back in. He was a postman; then became a Postal Inspector. My brothers didn't like the place; I did, except for the bugs! I have two brothers: Frederick, four years younger and George five years younger; but they didn't take to the water".

After many years away from Bear Lake, Martha, who lives in Fredonia in the winter, bought her current cottage in 1995 from the Brad and Marcia Sullivans [who now own the former Birmingham/Less cottages]. She often is seen in her kayak and hat out on the lake with friends. It's gratifying to see former Bear Lakers like the Martzs, Lanno/Foxes/Stengels/Mogfords exchange houses but remain on the lake or like Martha move back to the lake. A hard place to leave!

The Perkins/Hartmans: Note: In July of 2017, as we prepared to send this book to the publisher, Jane Perkins Cave, her husband and her brother James Perkins from California and Virginia, respectively, visited us at Bear Lake. They had summered at their grandparents' house on Bear Lake as children and came back to check out that house they had visited often. Their grandparents, Homer and Erma Perkins from Erie, PA bought a lot on the ridge going down to the lake from George Cooper and built a cottage there, which later became Brad and Marcia Sullivan's and is now the Wiser cottage. The Perkins' aunt and uncle were the Hartmans who had owned the Lamkin Store and boat livery across the street from it.

Jane and James shared anecdotes about living on the lake, among them about their grandfather *"going to Brocton and coming home with a large jar of brown liquid which, when poured on the ground, caused the nightcrawlers to come to the surface which were great for fishing."*

They also told us that the large 1939 photograph of two women with large muskies that hangs on the fireplace at Cabela's in Cheektowaga is actually of their mother, Marguerite Dickens Perkins and Ruth Ray. Jane's son, Brett Wingfield, was Cabela's Manager of Theme and Design at the time the store was built, and he chose to feature his grandmother in the Cheetowaga store. *"The photograph was enlarged from a very small original,"* according to Jane

It was fun to hear from still other early Bear Lake residents about life back then.

CHAPTER 15
SHADY REST: THE HISTORY
OF THE DEMING COTTAGE

This chapter offers a detailed account of the history of one Bear Lake cottage,"Shady Rest cottage," and the family that has lived in it the longest. The building of the cottage in 1924—1925 by George Reimann was described earlier in Chapter 3. Chapter 15 will provide a model for readers to use if they choose to write a history of their own cottages

The Demings have lived or summered in the Shady Rest Cottage at 8127 Bear Lake Road since 1978. Before them, the Coopers, Lamkins, Reimanns, Droneys, and Parrishes lived here or owned the property on which it was built. Long before the Coopers, Native Americans likely lived on this land. Tracing its history through its Title Search, United States Censuses and information provided by descendants of earlier and current owners from the 1890s to present day owners will provide readers with a template for their own histories .

Owners of property in Chautauqua County have a Title Search done when they purchase property. The one for 8127 Bear Lake Road is lengthy and starts with this description: *"That tract or parcel of land, situated in the Town of Pomfret, County of Chautauqua and State of New York and being part of Lot 50, in the 5ᵗʰ Township and 12ᵗʰ Range of the Holland Land Company's survey,"* which is consistent with the Holland Land Company information described in detail in an earlier chapter.

The first numbered item on the Deming Title Search begins the history of these properties by listing the death of Dulcena Cooper, intestate, on January 18, 1891 and the subsequent passing of her property (part of Lot 50) to the heirs-at-law, her children Eva Cooper Anscomb and George Cooper. Looking back into earlier United States Census records offers more about the Coopers. In the Census for 1860, for example, George Cooper is listed as *"2 years old, having been born about 1858,"* and his sister, Eva is listed as "4 ½." Their mother mentioned above was Dulcena (spelled in other Censuses as Dulcinia, and sometimes Delsena), and their father was John Cooper.

In the later 1870 Census, along with John and Dulcena and George and Eva, there is a John Cooper listed, who may have been George and Eva's grandfather and is most likely the "J. Cooper" listed as owning Lot 50 in the 1881 *Chautauqua County Atlas*. In that Census, a Sarah Cooper is also listed, probably George and Eva's grandmother since she appears later in the 1880 Census as being age seventy-one at that time.

Continuing through the Deming Title Search, on August 31, 1898, Eva Anscomb sold her share of her property in a quit-claim deed to her brother George for "$1.00 or more;" and on June 28, 1905, John Cooper (signing by "mark") conveyed another piece of property in a quit-claim deed, *"in consideration of $1.00 or more,"* to George Cooper. Again, it's not clear who this John Cooper is, but most likely he is George's father, John Cooper. In the early 1900s in the Title Search, George Cooper and Eva Cooper (Anscomb), granted various leases, to utility companies and granted lease-rents for fifty years to Carl J. Wolf, Edwin Wolf, and B. L. Fellows for property "upon which a Bungalow now stands," property next to one of the Deming lots. The Wolf family owned the land and cottage where the Wolf/Cave/Redden cottage now stands, and the Fellows family owned the land and cottage (called the "Kome Back Kottage) where the Fellows/Gilson/Loiocano/Scarborough cottage now stands. The Wolf cottage was on the east, and the Fellows cottage on the west side of where the Deming cottage would later stand, beginning in 1925.

The "Hang Out Cottage": Farther along in the Title Search, it is noted that on July 20, 1914, George and Eva Cooper leased land, a bungalow, (the Hang Out Cottage), and fifty feet of lake frontage to Mrs. Effa G. Young and Walter Lee Young. Later still, the Youngs leased that same property to Mrs. Walter Ensign. After Ensign on August 24, 1931 assigned her interest in the lease of that cottage to Alice Barber. Barber, in turn, on October 22, 1948 assigned the lease to George H. and Mary A. Parrish, then owners of Service Hardware in Dunkirk. The Hang Out Cottage, which no longer exists, was on Lot 11 (the lot closest to the Reddens), which was discerned because that lot's described dimensions, fifty feet by one hundred feet, is the size of the Deming's most easterly lot. In contrast, the other Deming lot # 10 has an irregular forty by one hundred twenty feet shape. Hang Out Cottage was located between the current Deming cottage and the Redden's cottage, but was no longer on Lot 11, nor were we able to find any photographs or descriptions of it when the Demings purchased Shady Rest and lots 10 and 11 from the Parrishes in 1977.

Lot 50: Back in May 17, 1924, George Cooper sold a part of Lot 50 to Silas T. Crocker. That land was located on Bear Lake Road where Cliff and Marie Couchman's house now stands. On July 1, 1925, after George Cooper had become a widower, he sold more land from Lot 50 and a cottage on the Bear Lake Road lakefront to Elizabeth L. Crocker. That Crocker cottage, east of the Redden's, fell into disrepair and was subsequently taken down by the Reddens after they purchased it from the Crocker estate.

The Title Search next lists the sale of Cooper property after George Cooper's death on April 29, 1934. On September 25, 1934, the adminstrator of Cooper's estate, Mary Hull Hipwell, sold "all that tract" (about one hundred and nine acres) to Walter W. and Edith M. (Cowden) Lamkin. After a description of the "premises," there's a two-page list of "excepting and reserving from the above described premises." These exceptions and reservations include all of those to whom George and Eva Cooper had deeded or leased property or utility leases on Lot 50. There is also a notation there about the sale of property and bungalows to the Crockers, (which are not, interestingly, listed as specific, individual property actions). All of the others previously listed in the title search are repeated as well.

Shady Rest Cottage: As for Lot 10, we find that Cooper sold *"all that tract"* to Ella T. Reimann, George Reimann's wife. Dick Birmingham, discussed in Chapter 3, confirms that his uncle, George S. Reimann, built the cottage that he called "Shady Rest" on a lot that he bought from George Cooper on September 12, 1924. That lot was bordered on the west by B. Fellows and on the east by Stanley Barber, and contained the Hang Out cottage that the Parrishes leased in 1948 before buying the Shady Rest cottage next door.

George Reimann began building his Shady Rest cottage in 1924 by clearing brush for it with his wife Ella (O'Brien) Reimann. Information on the construction of the cottage, also referenced earlier in the Reimann chapter, was gleaned from a journal that George kept for many years and that his daughter Mary Agnes still has. The authors are indebted to George for the colorful detail he provided us in his journal, and to Barbara Le Daniel, his great niece, for making it available to us. In it, George notes that his brother, Clarence and Clarence's wife Kathryn helped him and Ella build Shady Rest, but apparently never, themselves, owned property on Bear Lake. George and Clarence put in the piers for the cottage beginning in May of 1925. The lumber for them was cut down from the swamp forest further down Bear Lake Road. *"All logs were more than fifteen inches in diameter and seven feet long."* They used twelve of these piers to secure a foundation for a sixteen foot by twenty-four foot building. Work started on the cottage itself on July 24, 1925 with lumber purchased from Fredrickson Brothers in Cassadaga. The Reimann Journal also contained pictures of Shady Rest being built, and completed on August 2, 1925.

George, Ella, Mary Agnes and Robert Reimann at Shady Rest

Rebuilding Shady Rest & Adding a Veranda

George and his brother William added a veranda on the right front side of Shady Rest on July 5-9, 1926.

Shady Rest from the lakeside

Shady Rest from the Bear Lake Road side

Sometime, probably in 1949 when Brocton drained millions of gallons from Bear Lake for their reservoir, the land at the lake side was built up from the then available lake bed; and lake walls were built in front of several properties in Cob Cove (the area from the Johnstons to the Sullivans). One of Deming's walls (on Lot # 11) was a rock wall, the other (on Lot#10) a railroad tie wall.

The Reimanns and their children Robert and Mary Agnes moved to White Plains, New York in August of 1928, but visited their cottage annually. Sometime in the 1930s the cottage was lifted so that concrete piers could replace the original wooden ones, and beginning on September 9, 1947, two bedrooms were added on the north east side.

Lot 11 was eventually sold to George and Mary Parrish by Walter Lamkin in May of 1951. Lot 10 was sold to them by the executor of George Reimann's estate, Robert G. Reimann, for the sum of $2,200 in August of 1953.

The Parrishes sold the Shady Rest cottage and both lots 10 and 11 as one entity to the Demings on July 25, 1978. An additional narrow parcel that appears between the two lots on the survey was most likely a utility lease (which consequently required the purchase of title insurance).

For those of you who decide to trace the histories of your properties on Bear Lake, be prepared to engage in the same somewhat convoluted, detective work to unravel them as the Deming cottage history involved. Still it was and might be for you, fun to uncover. Not only will you learn a lot about your own cottages and property, but also about your neighbor's properties and owners of their cottages on Bear Lake.

Shady Rest Update: To bring the history of Shady Rest up to date, (of interest, perhaps only to the Demings), some changes in it and the family are added here. Although not closed on until 1978, the Parrishes offered and the Demings began using the cottage beginning in the Fall of 1977.

1979: The Dankert Brothers of Fredonia added a 12 x 22' deck onto the cottage.

1988: The usage of Shady Rest changed when Anne left her position at SUNY Fredonia, to accept a vice presidency at West Chester University in Pennsylvania. Mike and Maura had graduated from college and moved away, and Sean was in college in Atlanta. Bob began to summer where Anne was. In 1991 she moved again to become Vice President at Middle Tennessee State University. Bob (who continued to hug his tree at SUNY Fredonia) was the commuter in that eventual thirteen year commuter marriage which continued through Anne's vice presidency at Trinity University in DC and finally to her presidency at Notre Dame College in Cleveland. For two of those thirteen commuter years, Bob took a leave from SUNY to hold visiting professorships at Haverford College and Temple University and lived with Anne in West Chester, PA. For the other eleven years, he commuted to where she was every other weekend, at Christmas and other holidays and every summer after spring semester classes ended at SUNY Fredonia. During those years, the cottage was rented out.

Summer 1992: While in London (during Anne's Fulbright Fellowship there), Joe La Barbara of Fredonia remodeled and winterized the cottage following Bob's design. The floors were removed so that new concrete piers could be installed, supporting cross beams were reinforced and walls were removed and replaced. The lakeside windows were moved forward to the outside end of the screened porch to form a new outside wall; the bath was moved across the hall; the kitchen was completely redone; a laundry room was added toward the road; and the house was winterized, with baseboard heat, and a new woodburning stove was added. Emery Masiker constructed a ramp at road level for winter parking, when it would be too difficult to drive down the driveway. Returning from England that summer, Bob helped Joe complete the renovations and moved year-round to the cottage, where he lived for four years before moving back to

117

Fredonia (shoveling all that snow to get up to and down the stairs from the parking ramp every day got old!).

1992 Renovations: New entrance & laundry room

The 2000s: Bob spent the summers between 1989 and 200 wherever Anne lived, and the cottage was rented during many of those summers. The Demings and the Reddens nextdoor replaced their railroad tie lake walls with stones, a project engineered for them by Emery R Masiker and supervised diligently by the NY DEC. In 2000, Bob retired and joined Anne in Cleveland ending that long commuter experience. Married for 55 years now, "absence may have made their hearts grow fonder" as they say.

2003: Bruce Stonefoot of Fredonia expanded the cottage out the northwest side to include a new master bedroom and bath so that the extended family could all visit at once.

2004: A "Patio Enclosures" sunporch was constructed over the Dankert's deck to create a three seasons room.

2005: Stonefoot returned to add a deck beside the former deck/ now sunroom after the kids complained about not being able to sit outside on a deck.

2006: The failing three hundred gallon septic tank was replaced by the Masikers with a much larger fifteen hundred gallon tank, and a new leach field with sand filter was added. That year the Masikers also moved the shed back toward the north-west corner of the property. Over the years, the Masikers completed many projects at Shady Rest, including replacing the stone in our driveway and parking ramp multiple times and shoring up the lakewall.

2009: A second sunroom was added to the east side of the house after Stonefoot constructed a hallway to that sunroom from the kitchen using the closet space from one of the bedrooms. This second sunroom added much needed space for family reunions and for a gathering space for the five grandkids and cousins.

Shady Rest in Summer

2011: The area Amish have also been helpful. Amish builder Chris Shetler from Farr Road built and delivered a new twelve by fourteen feet shed constructed of Larch wood, and took the old one to his house to be used as a play house for his kids. Jake Nast, from Route 380, constructed the railing down the steps to the house from the parking ramp; and his wife made and sold us delicious Amish donuts every Friday for years ending in 2017. We are still experiencing withdrawal. Loved those donut.

2012: Patio Enclosures returned and put a roof over Bruce Stonefoot's deck because it was too hot to have lunch on the deck without it.

Shady Rest in winter

2003 to the present: Anne retired from Notre Dame College in June of 2003, and she and Bob moved to the Bear Lake cottage until their Cleveland house sold that November. They next moved to Wilmington Delaware where Mike's family lived and stayed for thirteen years. This past year (2017), they moved to Maris Grove, a retirement community near Wilmington in Glen Mills, PA. Since Anne's retirement in 2003, they have spent four months every summer at Shady Rest, where children Mike, Maura and Sean with spouses Denice and Jennifer and grandchildren Samantha, David, Liam, Owen and Siobhan visit annually and are sometimes joined by extended family members from Baltimore and Toronto.

Grandchildren at Bear Lake

Family Reunions

Bob, a certified Master Gardener, enjoys planting when they are at Bear Lake, because in their then Delaware townhouse community and now in the new community in PA, the gardening is done for them and planting anything is frowned upon. While Bob gardens, Anne collects outdoor sculpture for their Bear Lake property. Wooden outdoor sculptures from her stint in Tennessee and many metal pieces added since create a sculpture garden among Bob's plantings. The largest sculpture to date, a life-sized horse by Vince Freeman of Lakewood, was originally crafted to teach special needs kids to mount horses. When the therapeutic riding school, which had commissioned it, decided not to buy it after all, the Demings did. Their favorite piece, it has worked well for grandkid photos and often brings viewers down the driveway to give it a closer look. All are welcome! More recent sculptures were created by Chautauqua County Art Trail artists, some concrete or wood, but most of them metal, twelve of them to date by artist-welder Dale Anderson of Junktures in Forestville.

The Horse

The Demings hope to keep the ninety-eight year old Shady Rest cottage in their family to celebrate its 100th birthday in 2025 and maybe even for generations thereafter.

2017: marks the 40th year Demings have enjoyed Bear Lake.

2018: the year we will finally (after ten years) publish *A Bear Lake History* .

Our First Dale Anderson Purchase: The Anderson Heron

CHAPTER 16
THE BEAR LAKE PROPERTY OWNERS ASSOCIATION, INC. AND THE BEAR LAKE ASSOCIATION, INC.

The records of both the Bear Lake Property Owners Association and the subsequent Bear Lake Association are invaluable in tracing the lake's history. While archived records of Annual and Board Meetings from September 9, 1949 through July 14, 1984 exist, there are only scattered records from 1984 to 2005, but ample records again from 2006 to the present.

A Certificate of Incorporation of the Bear Lake Property Owners Association was filed with the State of New York, Department of State, Division of Corporations on September 9, 1949. The Association was formed in reaction to the Village of Brocton drawing down 116.7 million gallons of water from Bear Lake during the summer of 1949, which lowered the lake level, as one member described, "to a serious extent." At some time before 1949, Brocton had built a pump house to pump Bear Lake water for emergencies. By law, Brocton was allowed, in emergency situations, to draw 600,000 gallons a day from Bear Lake, but not millions of gallons. The Association hired the law firm of Kenneth W. Glines and Charles S. Collesano of Fredonia to file objections and to prevent Brocton from doing this again.

On September 30, 1949, Glines and Collesano notified the incorporators and members of the new organization that the Certification of Articles of Incorporation had been filed in Albany and in the County Clerk's Office at Mayville. Bylaws had been drafted and were ready for approval. A meeting of the members of the BLPOA was to be held Friday, October 7th at 8:00 p.m. for the purpose of adopting those bylaws and taking care of other Association business. The letter was addressed to fifty-one persons.

At that October 7th meeting the five "incorporators"—Walter W. Lamkin, John Rawson, Luther L. Pierce, Orval Brior, Hattie Sahle—signed the Certificate of Articles of Incorporation of the Bear Lake Property Owners Association (BLPOA). The Certificate was accepted by the members present; the five incorporators were recognized as the first directors of the BLPOA; the first officers: President Hattie Sahle, Vice President Walter Lamkin, Secretary Lena Brior and Treasurer Burnadette Gilbert were elected; and the bylaws were adopted. Glines & Collesano were directed to take *"such steps as will be necessary, proper and expedient toward protecting the interest of this Association in the matter of the use by the Village of Brocton of the waters of Bear Lake."* A bank account at the National Bank of Fredonia was authorized, and record books, books of account, stationary and office supplies were ordered.

The first meeting of the Board of Directors of the BLPOA was held on November 18, 1949. Kenneth Glines announced that the Fredonia Censor had completed printing the bylaws booklets (cost thirty dollars); that receipt books were printed by the Fredonia Censor (fourteen dollars and ten cents); and that aerial photographs of Bear Lake along with various communications were sent to the State Water Power and Control Commission in Albany (cost forty dollars to McLaren & McLaren for the aerial photographs). Discussion about the Brocton-Bear Lake water problem followed, and it was announced that Brocton had agreed to "clean up its reservoir" and had hired a Buffalo civil engineering firm to submit five plans to alleviate the present situation [of insufficient water], and that the Water Power and Control Commission would take steps in this matter, now held in abeyance until January 1, 1950 to permit Brocton to assemble its data and formulate plans.

The second meeting of the Board of Directors was held on May 19, 1950 at the Glines & Collesano office. In the discussion of the Brocton-Bear Lake water situation, Collesano reported that he had discussed the matter with J. C. Thompson of the Water Power and Control Commission in Albany on December 14, 1949. The matter had been referred to the Attorney General, and Collesano had appeared before the Brocton Village Board on April 3rd on this matter. The Village Board had no report from their civil engineers, but Brocton had taken steps to clean up its reservoir.

The first annual meeting for all of the members of the BLPOA was held on July 8, 1950, and an estimated seventy people attended. A letter from Glines & Collesano regarding the Brocton water situation was read (but a copy was not included with the minutes). The problem of Brocton taking water from Bear Lake continued as a major issue, but Glines & Collesano were as vigilant at staying on top of it as the property owners. Meetings were held by the local lawyers with representatives of the Water Power & Control Commission, and at the January 22, 1951 Board meeting, it was learned that Brocton was going to build a new dam and reservoir. The Board and members of the Association were concerned about where the Village would get its supply of water for same. They concurred that if the present reservoir on Burr Road were cleaned out, the storage capacity would be so increased that the Village of Brocton would not have to pump water from Bear Lake during the dry season of the year. The Board asked its attorneys to prepare a memorandum of objections to be filed before the February 1, 1951 hearing on the dam/reservoir project. At this point, the Board felt that they no longer needed the services of Glines & Collesano and decided to terminate the yearly contract with the lawyers.

Eventually the Village of Brocton was compelled to build a new reservoir with an eighty-four million gallons storage capacity at a cost of two hundred thousand dollars, but it was still drawing water from Bear Lake in 1954, the year its new reservoir came on line. Property owners were willing to *"swear by depositions"* that they heard the pump running and had seen water falling over the spill-way at the reservoir. Mr. Glines pointed out that the water piped from Bear Lake by-passes the reservoir, but said he would continue to check on the situation.

At the September 18, 1954 Board meeting, it was learned that the Village of Brocton was planning to supply Lake Erie State Park with water. Ray Frasier (then President) sent a letter of protest to the state Water Power & Control Commission. [That letter and its reply were read aloud at the Board meeting but were not included with the minutes of that meeting.] Glines and Collesano were again hired as the Board's representatives at any public hearing on this latest water project.

At a subsequent meeting of the Board on October 1, 1954, James Sommers (representing Glines & Collesano) reviewed the facts concerning the contract with Brocton, and stated that the law firm had received a letter from Mayor Fleming of Brocton stating that Brocton had not pumped water from Bear Lake except to clean their pumps. A public hearing on the Lake Erie State Park issue was scheduled for October 18, 1954, and Glines & Collesano and Association members were to attend, but no report of that meeting was found.

In 1967, the Village of Brocton wanted to enlarge its water district to include Portland, so the Association engaged Jim Sommers (of Glines and Collesano) to advise it about this pending problem. The Board met on March 25, 1967 to discuss two articles in the *Observer* about the Village's intent. At this meeting, Mr. Frasier, President, and Miss Crocker, Secretary, reviewed the history of the water problem with Brocton. They described *"the summer* [of 1949], *when so much water was withdrawn that it was necessary to walk out fifty feet to reach*

128

the water." Pictures were taken from the air [but unfortunately, no pictures were found], and the Secretary was instructed to contact Mr. Sommers (who was retained as counsel for the Association) concerning the situation and to write letters to the State Water Power & Control Commission and the Pomfret and Stockton Supervisors. On April 10, 1967, Mr. Sommers sent a letter to the Mayor of the Village of Brocton, and the two Supervisors and Boards of Pomfret, Portland, and Stockton as well as the New York State Water Resources Commission. Subsequently, a letter dated May 1, 1967 from the New York State Water Resources Commission was noted in the Board minutes stating that Portland would soon apply to take its water supply from Brocton. Sommers advised having a conference with John Luensman, County Planning Director, about the letter. A report of that meeting was read and attached to the minutes. [Unfortunately, it is not in the Archives.] In 1973, the Board again protested Brocton's selling water outside its Village limits and again in 1974 against extending its water district to Lake Erie.

Surveys of the Membership: Three surveys of the membership were sent out by the respective BLPOA presidents over the years. The first in 1954 was sent out by President Ray Frasier attempting to get feedback for or against the proposed dam and reservoir. The second survey, sent out by President Nancy Schifferli in 1965 asked for feedback on: *"street lights (six votes for), public phone booth (nineteen votes for), garbage collection (twelve votes for), appointed Constable (ten votes for), weed and pollution control (eighteen and twenty votes for respectively), and other suggestions."* Sixty-two surveys were sent out; twenty-six were returned.

The third survey was sent out in August of 1981 by President Dick Birmingham, asking four questions: *"1. Should a speed limit be imposed on boats using Bear Lake: twenty-seven said 'yes,' twelve said 'no,' and the average speed limit was suggested at thirty mph; 2. Should a horsepower limit be imposed on engines on boats: twenty-four said 'yes,' fourteen said 'no,' and the average horsepower limit suggested was fifty hp.; 3. Should the speed limit on Bear Lake Road be reduced during the summer months: twenty-four said 'yes,' sixteen said 'no,' and the average speed limit suggested was twenty-five mph; 4. Should there be a leash law for dogs: twenty said 'yes,' twenty said 'no.'* [There is no record of the implementation of these responses, but speed limits and boat horse power were topics at many later meetings with no action.]

Newsletter: A Bear Lake Newsletter was first proposed at a Board meeting on August 1, 1976, and LeRoy Goldhardt offered to draft one. At a Board meeting on July 24, 1983, it was suggested that the Newsletter come out twice a year. It looks like there was a hiatus for many years until Cathye Mogford and then Deb Lanni started it again around 2002. Bob Deming continued it from 2012 to 2017 when Steve Latko took it over.

Bylaws: Revising the bylaws was mentioned several times in the minutes of Board meetings, but not actually accomplished until 1974. A special meeting was called for Saturday, August 31st of that year to consider revisions, the principal areas of modification being: *Article II, Section 1: increase in the size of the Board from five to nine; Section II: addition of grievance procedures; Article III, Section 1: change from elected to appointed officers; Article IV, Section 1: extension of privileges of membership to members of immediate family of property owner; Section 4: July 15th set as deadline for payment of dues.* The 1974 Bylaws remained applicable until the 2010 revisions and the more extensive July 2012 revisions when the Association name and purposes changed, which will be discussed later in this chapter .

The Twenty-Fifth Anniversary of the BLPOA: In anticipation of the anniversary of the BLPOA in 1975, a "Sunshine Committee" was appointed in 1974 consisting of Judy Bogner, Kay Orloff, Dorothy Steff, Marsha Sullivan and Ann Berndt to prepare a celebration. At the twenty-fifth Anniversary Annual Meeting and picnic on July 26, 1975, it was reported that the YMCA Camp was for sale for an asking price of one hundred fifty thousand dollars. Dick Birmingham talked to State officials about this sale, and they suggested three alternatives: 1. apply to the Wetland Acquisition Program (which apparently had no funds); 2. acquire the property for public access to the lake (but the size and price preclude any possibility of this); 3. have the State acquire the first one hundred yards or so of shoreline to protect the ecology of the lake (if it can be demonstrated to them that this is necessary). Birmingham was to draft a letter to the State to persuade them to take action while Federal or County solutions were being investigated. One of the suggestions offered at the time was to turn the Y Camp into a Bird Sanctuary, and Birmingham was asked to investigate the legislative rules on waterways and environmental dedication of wilderness areas for such a purpose by the State of New York. Efforts continue to be taken to preserve the ecology of the lake with approaches to the current owner and to not for profit organizations. Anne Deming also tried often but unsuccessfully to do so beginning in 2015.

It was also announced at that meeting that the Masiker family was selling land next to the store to the State for a small boat launch. When done, the State will resume stocking the lake with fish as they had in past years. Sixty-three people attended the twenty-fifth Anniversary Annual Meeting.

[There are no Association minutes or notes in the Archives for the period 1975-1979. There are some minutes for the 1980-1984 period, but none for the 1985 through 2007 period. An unsuccessful effort was made to recover those materials.]

The Not-for-Profit Status of the BLPOA: The Archives contain the papers that had been drawn up for acquiring a certificate of not-for-profit corporation status as early as 1974, but they were not signed. Nor is there any document in the Archives indicating that the BLPOA received not-for-profit status. There is a letter dated July 11, 1972 to the Association from Francis Persen, Chief, Instructions and Interpretations Unit of the State Tax Commission, suggesting it would not have qualified: *"It has been determined that your organization is not entitled to exemption* [from the New York State and local sales and use tax] *since you are not organized and operated exclusively for one or more of the purposes outlined above.—'Any corporation, association, trust, or community chest, fund or foundation, organized and operated exclusively for religious, charitable, scientific, testing for public safety, literary or educational purposes. . . .'"* The letter from Mr. Persen continues: *"While a portion of your activities may be for such purpose, you are primarily operated for civic and recreational and social purposes."* The Association did, however, have a Tax Identification Number (16-1267821); and the NYS Department of State (on its website) listed the BLPOA, Inc. as a "Domestic Not-for-Profit Corporation.

In 2008, the Board approved applying for 501©3 status for the Association in order for it to seek tax-advantaged funding from corporations, foundations and individuals, like Cassadaga, Findley and Chautauqu Lake Association do. After a long time completing it, but before mailing it, Deming called the IRS to assure its mission would be approved, and was informed that the Association would not be eligible for 501©3 status unless the purposes stated in the 1949 incorporation certificate were amended to include what the Association currently does, which fits eligibility and not what we said we would do back then, but have never done.

In 1949, the Association was incorporated *"as a recreational center and summer colony* and listed ambitious purposes which were never achieved, among them *"the development of Bear Lake including the securing, construction and maintenance of parks and playgrounds, sewage, sanitation, light, heat, power, water, fire and police protection and assemblies for musical entertainment along educational, scientific, musical, recreational and other lines for its members . . . ."* Not fulfilling these purposes, the Association has, instead, concentrated solely on preserving the health and welfare of the lake by treating invasive weeds, attempting to control boat speed, assuring the safety of the water for swimming and fishing and occasionally bringing in educational speakers to address water quality issues, all of which the IRS advised Deming serve to "lesson the burden of the government to do so" and thereby do qualify the Association for 501c3 status as a public charity. The IRS also recommended that the name of the Association be changed to the Bear Lake Association since for some time it had not been open exclusively to property owners. For example, the Conservation Club, all renters, has been an ex-officio member for many years, and S.C.O.R.E and the Cassadaga Lakes Association are also members. In order to apply for this public charity status, Deming prepared a document to amend the 1949 incorporation certificate, which the Board approved and sent to the full membership for approval at its Annual meeting. The recommended new language included: *"1. The name of the proposed corporation shall be Bear Lake Association, Incorporated. 2. The purposes for which it is to be formed are to maintain and preserve Bear Lake and its watershed in the towns of Pomfret and Stockton, Chautauqua County, New York for the benefit of all Bear Lake users, by promoting and facilitating scientific lake studies, weed control, water quality testing and the education of the community about Bear Lake's ecosystem and environmental lake management, thereby lessening the burden of state, county and town to do so."* The bylaws of the association were amended to align with the new wording of the Certificate of Incorporation.

These changes were unanimously approved by the BLPOA members at the Annual Meeting in July of 2012. The amendment of the certificate of incorporation was submitted to the New York Department of State for approval, but, unfortunately, it came back multiple times not approved as submitted, for seemingly trivial reasons, one of which was the name of the Association needed to be in all capital letters. Frustrated by the many changes, none of which satisfied the Department of State, the Board hired attorney Neil Robinson, to review it, make necessary corrections and resubmit it. Even after his changes, it was rejected twice. After two years of submissions and rejections, in July of 2014, New York modified its incorporation laws, making application for not-for-profit status easier. Robinson recommended that instead of continuing to try to get the old incorporation amended, the Association would be better served by applying for a totally new incorporation. The Board agreed and the application for The Bear Lake Association, Inc. was again submitted and finally approved by the Department of State on November 12, 2014, thereby replacing the former Bear Lake Property Owners Association. Inc. with the new name, Bear Lake Association, Inc. With a new corporation in place, the Board applied for federal 501©3 status. Federal form 1023EZ was submitted to the federal Department of Revenue; and the Bear Lake Association Inc. was approved on May 19, 2015, effective retroactively to the date of incorporation, November 14, 2014.

Grants: Grants have supported the Association's weed control efforts and bio control program since 2007. Deming applied for and received the Associations first grant in 2007, a three year state grant of nine thousand dollars facilitated by Senator Catherine Young, which was used to rent the Cassadaga Lake harvester for two years and then used for the establishment and implementation of our Lake Management Plan and the beginning of our bio control program in the third year, the year in which the additional three thousand indigenous weevils were introduced into the lake. The bio control program is discussed in Chapter 18.

Bed tax grants were applied for and awarded for four thousand dollars in 2011, and a second one for five thousand dollars in 2013 was then extended through 2014 and 2015 when all of the funds had not expended. Each of the grants supported water quality improvements and weed control and allowed the Association to continue to use the services of researcher, Dr. Robert Johnson, formerly of Cornell University and now of Racine Johnson Aquatic Ecologists, to guide our efforts. To supplement the weevils added in 2010, using funds from our 2013 bed tax grant, Dr. Johnson also increased the indigenous moth population in the lake. To date, only one of the Association's County Bed Tax or Occupancy Grant applications was not ranked high enough to be funded. Further grant and fundraising efforts awaited approval of the NY incorporation of the "new" Association (i.e., Bear Lake Association, Inc.) and the receiving of the 501©3 status; both of which as of 2015 are now extant. With this status, funding from governmental sources can now be supplemented by tax advantaged funding from individuals, corporations and foundations.

The largest grant to benefit Bear Lake was received in June of 2015. Managed by the Chautauqua County Soil & Water Department, one hundred thousand dollars was awarded by the State for Bear Lake weed control and dredging. A comprehensive and updated Management Plan is in progress and dredging is in the planning stages to be funded by this grant.

County Allocation Increases: Deming's 2013 appeal to the county to increase the Association's annual allocation to control invasive weeds was successful, granting the Association one thousand five hundred dollars annually, up from seven hundred and fifty dollars in 2012 and five hundred dollars annually before then. The Association has also been supported annually with five hundred dollar grants from the towns of Stockton and Pomfret.

Water Testing: The Board began a water testing program in 2011 to assure the safety of the lake for swimming, fishing and other recreational activities. Charged sixteen dollars per water sample, the samples had to be submitted to Mayville within six hours of being taken. The Board considered the expense warranted to assure that the many children swimming in the lake are swimming in clean water. Roger Britz collected the samples three times each summer from 2011 until 2017, when students from SUNY Fredonia, Environmental Science Department assumed that responsibility, offering water testing at no cost. Since initiating this program in 2011, all tests have shown the lake to be safe and the water of high quality.

Much has been accomplished since the establishment of the Association in 1949. The Association remains strong today.

CHAPTER 17
OTHER BEAR LAKE EVENTS AND ISSUES

E vents and issues that have affected or might affect Bear Lake in the future, from septic inspections to new fauna and flora, are covered in this chapter.

The Chautauqua County Navigation Commission (CCNC), created by passage of Chapter 780 of the County Laws of 1950, held a public hearing covering proposed rules for Chautauqua, Cassadaga, and Bear Lake at the County Court House on August 7, 1950; but the Commission did not adopt any rules or regulations until the opening of navigation in the spring of 1951. Bear Lake Association secretaries wrote to the Commission and other agencies pointing out that the rules and regulations were not, in many instances, applicable to Bear Lake.

At the request of BLPOA President Frasier on March 22, 1951, Secretary Brior sent a copy of the suggested proposed rules for Bear Lake to Joseph H. Dornberger, President, CCNC, noting that the rules had been approved by Mr. Tanner, Supervisor of the Town of Stockton and Victor Sawkins who were "present at the meeting" of the Bear Lake Committee that drafted the rules: The Proposed Rules for Bear Lake included: *"1. All power operated boats shall be registrered; 2. No person shall navigate or operate a boat in a manner which unreasonably interferes with the free and proper use of the waters of Bear Lake, or unreasonably endangers the users of the Lake. Reckless navigation and, or, operation is not permitted; 3. All boat operators shall be responsible for their own wake. Boats operated by persons under 16 years of age shall be operated only with the consent of the owners who assume full responsibility; 4. All boats and canoes in use on the waters of Bear Lake between the hours of one-half hour after sunset and one-half hour before sunrise shall be provided with a light to be displayed upon the approach of any other boat or canoe within the distance of 200 feet."* In 1952, following letters to the Town of Pomfret Supervisor, Bear Lake was exempted from the Navigation laws.

Fire Districts and Fire Protection: Sometime before 1953, according to a memo in the Archives authored by the Secretary, four plots of land, one of which included Bear Lake, were voted out of the Town of Pomfret fire protection district. *"As a result, if Fredonia were called,"* the memo states, *"it would be solely up to the chiefs since the insurance of the department would not cover them out of the district."* At a February 16, 1953 BLPOA Board meeting, the Directors discussed having their own fire equipment, and a Fire Committee including Messers Elliott, Lamkin, Case and Rawson was established to investigate that option,. At the next Board meeting, March 16, 1953, the Fire Committee reported on its meeting with Chief and Assistant Chief of the Fredonia Fire Department at which the Committee was strongly advised not to purchase its own fire equipment because the insurance rates would be too high, there would be a problem as to where to keep the equipment, and another problem regarding where to store the fire hose until it dried out. No further action was taken. Years later, Arden Berndt, a member of the Stockton Fire Department, reported at the Board meeting on June 25, 1968 that Stockton would like to have Bear Lake in its fire protection district. The Board decided to stay with the Fredonia Fire Department.

Street Lighting: Sometime during the summer months of 1953, President Raymond Frasier wrote to Supervisor Strubing of

Dunkirk about installing street lights along the county road. Robert M. Howard, who was then Acting County Superintendent for Highways, wrote to Frasier noting *that "the County has never to my knowledge provided for the installation or maintenance of street lights on any County highway."* In response to a later letter from John Sahle requesting establishing a "street lighting district," a letter dated May 20, 1954 from Niagara Mohawk Power Corporation indicates that they would install thirteen thousand two hundred and fifty lumen bare lamps at the average spacing of four hundred eighty-seven feet between the Stockton-Bear Lake Road intersection and the Basket Factory leading to the annual charges of $418.13, which would be raised by *"direct taxation of the property owners within the lighting district boundary."* The Board declined the offer.

On May 29, 1971 Secretary Shirley Thorp wrote to Supervisors in both townships requesting that a *"vapor light"* be installed at the intersection of Bear Lake Road and Town Line Road. Evelyn Lindsay, Town Clerk for Pomfret, wrote back on June 8, 1971 that the Town Board had approved the request and Niagara Mohawk would be installing the light *"in the very near future."*

Hydro-Electric Plant: On December 8, 1953, the Energy Accumulation and Exchange Corporation (Accumex) filed a declaration of intent with the Federal Power Commission to construct a hydroelectric plant on the shore of Lake Erie near the Village of Brocton. The electric generators at the plant would be driven by water coursing down the escarpment through ten foot or twelve foot penstocks from two artificial reservoirs created by *"closing a valley called either Bear Lake Valley or Stockton Valley, the reservoir having an area of some 7,000 acres."* Water was to be pumped from Lake Erie up the escarpment into the valley reservoirs. A public hearing was set for February 15, 1954 after the declaration was posted at local post offices. Representatives of the Town of Stockton and residents of Bear Lake and Cassadaga Lake were invited to the hearing. Letters of protest were initiated by Raymond Frasier, President, and sent to local officials. Frasier's letter from the Power Authority noted that Accumex had not yet filed an application for the Bear Lake Valley Project. Frasier's response from the Water Power and Control Commission noted that their only information came from the declaration, from various newspaper articles *"originating in your locality and from people such as yourself."* They also suggested hiring an attorney to represent property owners' interests.

A letter in the archives file from W. A. Birmingham to Raymond Frasier states his "absolute opposition" to the project. Birmingham had enlisted the help of Congressman Reed (a letter from Reed to Birmingham is also in the file) as soon as Birmingham heard news of the project. He mentions an article about the project in the *Buffalo Evening News* for March 3, 1954. The project did not happen.

Speed Limits on Bear Lake Road: As early as July of 1955, Secretary Elizabeth Crocker wrote to the County Road Commissioner, Robert Howard, about the high rate of speed being used by drivers along the road passing Bear Lake and requesting that fifteen miles per hour signs be posted like those at the Cassadaga Community Park. Mr. Howard responded in a letter dated August 3, 1955, that there was currently a thirty mph sign posted, pursuant to the State Traffic Commission; that he does not have the power or authority to alter speeds established by the Traffic Commission; and that the speed limit at the Cassadaga Park was set by the Village Board, which has authority over roads in an incorporated village. In 2013, President Deming asked county representative John Runkle if the thirty MPH sign coming toward the lake from Brocton could be moved closer to the lake. He contacted the DOT about it, but he indicated that he did not have jurisdiction over a state road. Eventually in 2014, two additional signs were installed at each end of the lake which the Association paid for. As of 2017, the speed limit has yet to change, but in 2014, "little green men to slow traffic" and additional thirty mph signs with orange tags on them were added, purchased by the BLA.

The Dump: At the Board meeting on July 18, 1957, Walter Lamkin reported that people or residents other than members of the Association were using the dumping ground across from the Basket Factory. A "Keep Out" sign for that area was requested; and at the Board meeting on July 14, 1962, a house-to-house canvas for contributions was suggested for the dump fund. Later it was determined that anyone with a Stockton address could purchase for a dollar a Stockton dump permit from the Town Clerk to use the Stockton Dump. The Lamkin dump then closed.

Gas Line: At a December 7, 1950 Board meeting, President Frasier reported that he had contacted the Gas Company, and that it would cost fifteen thousand dollars to lay gas pipe from Stockton to Bear Lake. Additionally, a 2 percent surcharge on half of the fifteen thousand dollars would be assessed on consumers until such time as revenue collection amounted to four hundred fifty dollars per year for two consecutive years. No further action was taken on the gas line issue.

Telephone Lines and an Outside Telephone: In response to a letter in 1959 from Secretary Elizabeth Crocker to Robert Maytum of the Dunkirk & Fredonia Telephone Company, requesting more than the two-line, multi-party telephone lines along the lake, Roderick A. Nixon of the Chautauqua & Erie Telephone Corporation answered that there are several applications for additional service, and one will be given service very shortly. A letter dated June 27, 1966 from President David Dorman to the C&ETC repeats an earlier request that a phone booth be installed at Masiker's store. No answer was received, but a phone booth was installed shortly after sending his letter, (according to a handwritten note on the bottom of the copy of Dorman's letter).

Mobile Homes: At several Board meetings, the matter of mobile homes was discussed. At a meeting on April 24, 1967, it was noted that one or two more will probably be moved onto the former Foote-Campbell property on the south east side of the lake in the Town of Stockton. Mr. McClelland was delegated to look further into the zoning laws of the Town of Pomfret. In 2016, a mobile home was required to be moved from a lakefront property by the Town of Pomfret Zoning Board of Appeals.

Mosquito Spraying: Mosquito spraying took place once or twice a season as early as 1968. The spray was a DDT solution at the cost of three to four dollars per property owner when done as a whole. In June of 1968, spraying took place and a second spraying took place after being authorized at the BLPOA Annual Meeting that year. A third spraying at Muskie Point was also noted. Fred Carr reported using Methoxychor, a DDT substitute which doesn't harm birds or animals but is harmful to fish. By 1970 the cost of spraying had increased. In 1972 the Conservation Club offered one hundred twenty-five dollars to help financially with its cost of spraying. The sprayer was sold in the early 1980s.

Road Conditions: In March of 1967, Joseph Henry, County Highway Commissioner was contacted about the condition of South Town Line Road. A similar letter was addressed to Stewart Dudley, Town of Pomfret Supervisor, who responded quickly to Ms. Crocker's letter telling her he had forwarded her letter to Mr. Henry, who informed Mr. Dudley that *"he is aware of the deplorable situation and temporary measures to alleviate the situation have been undertaken."*

Open Space Plan: On behalf of the Bear Lake Association, President Anne Deming sent a letter in 2013 to the New York Open Space Plan Committee requesting that Bear Lake be kept in their 2014 plan. With over 70 percent of the land surrounding Bear Lake undeveloped, making it the largest wetland in the county, it warranted priority among conservation projects, she argued. The letter also documented for the Committee how the Bear Lake Association *"had established a Lake Management Plan and put in place a bio control program for controlling invasive weeds and annual water testing to assure that the lake is safe for swimming and fishing. The only lake in Chautauqua County to use bio control exclusively, in 2014 then its fifth year, the program has proven very effective at controlling both Eurasian Milfoil and toxic algae, resulting in very few weeds and no blue green algae,"*

Her letter was also read at the New York Department of Environmental Conservation (DEC) Open Space Plan public meeting. Board member, Bernie Klaich, attended that meeting and reported that several Chautauqua Lake Association members in attendance, including Jane Conroe, a friend of the Demings, supported the appeal. In the fall of 2013, John Bartlett from the Foundation for Sustainable Forests had contacted President Deming requesting a tour of Bear Lake to assess its importance to his organization. Back in Delaware then, she contacted Sid Potsmesil, Second Vice President, who took Bartlett out on the lake, where he took many photos and reported back that he was very impressed and felt strongly that Bear Lake should be included in the Open Space Plan. Bartlett followed that report with a letter to the Open Space Committee hearing supporting the preservation of Bear Lake and its watershed. Bartlett and Conroe were sent letters of appreciation for their support, and Bear Lake was ultimately included in the New York Open Space Plan as a priority in 2014.

A TMDL Plan for Bear Lake: Following a mandate from the United States Environmental Protection Agency, the New York Department of Environmental Conservation (NYDEC) prepared a Total Maximum Daily Load plan for Bear Lake. One benefit of having a TMDL plan would be to open Bear Lake up for grant money to improve water quality. *"In any case, it looks like it could be a good thing, and we apparently do not have any right to stop it even if it weren't,"* said Deming. Dr. Steven Gladding, Environmental Engineer in the NYDEC Water Quality Management Division, explained further that TMDL would *"determine the maximum allowable amount of a pollutant that may enter a water body in order for that water body to still meet water quality standards. In essence, this TMDL will place a cap on the amount of phosphorus that may enter Bear Lake. The TMDL process is used to set permit limits for point source discharges and to specify the amount of reduction needed from non-point sources. DEC and U.S. EPA have very limited regulatory authority over non-point sources. In the Bear Lake watershed, there are no point source discharges, and the two main non-point sources of phosphorus are agriculture and septic systems. The TMDL will determine the amount of load reduction needed, but implementation will rely upon voluntary implementation. Bear Lake is listed on the NYS 303(d) list of impaired waters due to nutrients (phosphorus) with the identified source as agriculture"*

The proposed DEC Bear Lake TMDL plan was provided to residents in the June 2014 *Bear Lake Newsletter* and discussed at the Annual Meeting in July. DEC's Draft plan, issued on July 23, 2014, was made available online for review and comment; and a public meeting to discuss the draft was held on Thursday, August 14, 2014 at the Stockton Volunteer Fire Hall. Notice of the meeting was sent to Bear Lake permanent residents and other local interest groups, including town supervisors and Departments of Health and Soil & Water. Notice was not, however, sent to summer residents for some reason. More specific questions regarding the implementation of the plan were covered at the August 14 meeting which was attended by approximately twenty people, many of them Bear Lake Association members.

At that August meeting, Gladding explained the draft TMDL for Bear Lake, and the plan to limit the amount of nutrients entering the lake to meet water quality standards. He explained that Bear Lake is a *"Class A lake because it is a water source for Brocton for drinking water"* [despite the fact that it has not been used for that purpose for many years]. Chautauqua Lake is also Class A while Cassadaga and Findley lakes are Class B, recreation lakes.

Several Bear Lake residents at the meeting raised objections to the TMDL draft plan during the question and answer period, including one who questioned why DEC waited from 1998 (when the lake was declared "impaired") to now, in 2014, to make its recommendations; he received no clear answer. Others questioned why so much of the data used in the Report were out of date (for example, only 2006 and 2012 levels of phosphorous were used) and some of the data was from as long ago as 2001. The Report noted that "local knowledge" about the Lake was gathered where available, but no one locally had been contacted while the Draft Report was being developed. Anne Deming had submitted a Board-approved two page critique of the draft before the public meeting relaying concerns and questions regarding it to be included as part of the written responses to the Report due to the DEC by Friday, August 22nd. After repeating several times at the meeting that implementation of the DEC recommendations for phosphorous load reductions was "voluntary," Gladding noted that neither DEC nor the EPA can enforce those recommendations; enforcement rests with the County Health Department. As Deming summarized *"all of us on Bear Lake and the DEC have the best interests of the lake at heart, but the faulty data used to develop this draft*

TMDL plan need to be rectified for it to be accepted as a viable plan to improve the lake."

Gladding agreed that the Association would be sent a revised Draft Report, after the outdated and erroneous data were corrected. Following the meeting, the Board sent a formal request for an extension of the comment period, as did several individual residents, and Gladding subsequently agreed to an extended open period for discussion until the end of the first week in September.

In February of 2015, a revised TMDL draft was issued by the DEC, and several members of the BLA Board participated in a conference call discussing the changes in it. Unfortunately, the DEC's February 2015 revision of the TMDL reflected very few of the changes suggested in the earlier TMDL draft of July 2014, at the public hearing on August 14, 2014, or at the open period for public comment lasting until September 5th. A few corrections of data in the earlier draft were made as a result of vigorous challenges by the Bear Lake Association President, Secretary, and several Board members. For example, DEC acknowledged the existence of two campgrounds with their own holding tanks that do not discharge into the lake, which their research group, The Cadmus Group, did not know about. This resulted in lowering the pounds of Phosphorus presumably put into the lake by septic systems from fifty-five to fifty point two pounds—totaling 11.5 percent of the total phosphorus loading to the lake. The number of residences on the lake was also revised (the TMDL had 80 percent of the residents as year round residents when only 20 percent of them are, a serious error). The Report continues to indicate that Bear Lake has "degraded water quality due to excessive weed and algae growth . . . ," but the Report did not take into account any of the results of the Association's biocontrol program which had considerably improved the water quality and reduced the weeds and algae growth since its implementation in 2010 and in annual monitoring since then. The annual water quality testing has also always given positive results for water quality.

Additional incorrect data were still used as a basis for the TMDL Report. DEC's demographic data reported that there are fifteen houses within fifty feet of the shore land, when there are only eleven. Among those houses, three of them have not been lived in for many years, information which would clearly affect septic system loading. The primary recommendation that the DEC offered for correction of the phosphorous load was to install a sewer treatment facility or connect to an existing treatment facility, at a cost of two to three million and requiring town, county, and state funding, far too costly a solution for Bear Lake with so few year-round residents. Enforcement of the TMDL is to be the responsibility of the understaffed County Health Department. It is assumed that the February 2015 DEC TMDL report has now been forwarded to the Federal EPA. By 2015, the Health Department had mandated faulty septic system corrections and replacement at Bear Lake; and the septic systems involved are currently in the process of being corrected.

Bear Lake Fish: In 1952, a representative from the County Federation was expected to survey and study the fish situation in Bear Lake. At a June 25, 1968 Board meeting, it was reported that the Conservation Department had stocked three hundred muskie fry in 1967. In early June, 2013, President Deming queried the DEC about fish shocking in the lake and got a response from Justin Brewer with the NYSDEC Bureau of fisheries in Region 9, stating that they were doing a survey as part of an Allegheny River drainage fish community assessment. Because Bear lake is part of that drainage, they did the sampling to get an idea of the fish community. They caught *"black crappie, largemouth bass, bluegill, pumpkinseed, grass pickerel, muskellunge, brown bullhead, carp, and gold shiner."* Although they did not do an assessment of the entire lake, they reported that the fish numbers seemed *"fine and plentiful."*

Brewer added that certain bodies of water have specific habitats to support specific fish. *"Bear Lake, having a healthy population of bass and musky would not be a good place to stock other fish because the effects of predation would most likely eliminate the stocked fish."* When asked why Walleye were not stocked, he suggested that *"over the years they have found the habitat in the lake to be more suitable for musky and the survival of walleye would most likely be very poor in Bear lake."* In a later update, Michael Clancy of DEC sent President Deming a message saying that walleye are stocked in Bear Lake every other year, with two thousand three hundred fingerlings stocked in 2013. Five hundred fifty Muskies are stocked each year in mid to late September and Brown Trout are stocked in the Outlet. In 2015, seven hundred seventy Brown Trout were stocked in the Outlet.

Chuck Battaglia, former Cassadaga Lake Manager, requested a donation from the Bear Lake Association to defray the cost of increasing the size of fingerlings before stocking Bear Lake. The Board agreed that this was a worthwhile endeavor and sent fifty dollars to support the Prendergast Hatchery. Chuck explained: *"The NYSDEC Prendergast Hatchery is responsible for all the Musky stocking in NY. Last year, 550 8" muskies were stocked in Bear Lake in the fall. Thanks to our feedings, they grew an extra 2+ inches over what the State was able to grow them because of budget restraints, and had a much better chance of survival."*

Organizational Members: The Cassadaga Lakes Association joined the Bear Lake Association as a member. Bear Lake Association has been a member of their association for several years and invited them to join BLA, in turn, so that the associations can support each other. Back in 2009, President Deming wrote a letter on behalf of the BLA to Senator Catherine Young on behalf of the Cassadaga Lakes Association to support their appeal for state funding to buy a new harvester. The Bear Lake

Association is also a member of S.C.O.R.E, the Stockton beau-
tification group. The reciprocal memberships may be helpful
to Bear Lake.

Sandy: And then there was "Sandy." On October 29, 2012,
Hurricane Sandy caused Bear Lake to flood extensively with
the lake up to the highest it's been since 1972, according to
a longtime resident. The then Clever's campground and the
Conservation Club areas were "completely inundated by water."
Clever was quoted in the October 31st issue of the *Post Journal*
and press coverage in the *Observer* also included photos of the
flooding on the Northwest end showing the Deming property
with high water, but fortunately had none inside, the Loiocano
cottage next door with at least a foot of water inside, and
water under the Britz cottage. At midlake, the Dobbins were
missing two dock pieces, made of composite and wood and two
unclaimed picnic tables had arrived on the shore line opposite
their driveway. The Conservation Club was missing a fourteen
foot aluminum rowboat.

The YMCA/Hornburg Property: When the Hornburg prop
erty was listed for sale in 2012, President Deming sent a letter
to the President of the Chautauqua Watershed Conservancy
to request that the Conservancy consider buying or securing
a donation of the property so that it could be conserved as a
wildlife preserve with its Great Blue Herons (and more recent
American Eagles), mink and beavers inhabiting it. Interested,
John Jablonski, Executive Director of the Conservancy, made
contact with the owners and also secured additional interest
from the Nature Conservancy, the Foundation for Sustainable
Forests, the Sierra Club and Ducks Unlimited to work together
to try to conserve it.

Owned originally by Clifford Pierce, (discussed in Chapter
11) who had donated some of his property to the YMCA for
a camp, Walter Hornburg of Sinclairville later bought that

entire property, logged it and built a house on it. Within a few years, he took the house down and put the property up for sale. Information on the property collected by John Jablonski for the conservation project, included: *"311 acres +/-;with an appraised value of $450,000 in 2012 including a current oil/gas lease. It is the largest undeveloped shoreline area on Bear Lake, or on any Chautauqua County lake; one of the largest wetlands in Chautauqua County with 20 to 30 acres of Maple-Ash Palustrine Forest. A biological survey was incomplete, but there was the potential of rare and/or endangered plants."*

The Bear Lake Association also contacted legislators and others to see if there was any way that they might secure at least the waterfront acreage. Senator Catherine Young responded that the DEC had informed her that there is a DEC Wildlife Program and that they would visit to determine if the property fits their goals. The property was not, however, she said a "high priority" for the DEC. Others responding to Deming's letter include Assemblyman Goodell, Lorin Cornell of Governor Cumo's office, Jeff Mapes, Steven Gladding, Jeff Nyitrai and Paul McKeown all of the DEC. County Legislator John Runkel was also contacted as was Legislator George Borrello who was helpful to us in the past.

After years of trying unsuccessfully to get the land conserved to no avail, the Hornburg property was purchased by Dennis Sabella in 2014, owner of a lumber manufacturing company in Tidioute, PA. Mr. Sabella was approached directly by President Deming after the sale was concluded. She explained the bio control program and the Board's concern that disturbing the waterfront could negate years of efforts to control the weeds. [The weevils winter on that lakefront.] Very graciously, he called her to assure her that he *"did not destroy forests or land because he cares about them,"* and told her that he had no immediate plans to log the former Hornburg site and, indeed, probably would not do anything with the property *"before twenty years, if then."* Elated, Deming welcomed him to Bear Lake, sent him the 2014 Bear

Lake *Newsletters* and offered to host him for a drink and tour of the lake when she and Bob returned in the summer of 2015. He still receives the *Newsletter* yearly. The Board continues to this day its efforts to find a way to conserve the property abutting the Lake.

The Fishers are Here: Bob and Lyn Dee Dobbins' woodlot on Chautauqua Road was one of 608 statewide sites in 2014 that the DEC used to survey the presence of Fishers (also called Fisher Cats) in our area. Fishers are five to fifteen pound mammals, members of the weasel family, with sharp pointy teeth, but are not harmful to humans. They have suddenly appeared throughout the Southern Tier, migrating here probably from Pennsylvania.

A Fisher Cat on Dobbins woodlot

They inhabit the heavily wooded areas and feed on small animals. DEC built bait sites with adjacent cameras, and the Dobbins were supplied with a CD disk showing the fishers visiting the site on their woodlot. On May 29, 2015, the Dobbins were sent another CD from the DEC, which showed no Fishers spotted on camera over the past year, which they said could have been because of deep snow. The DEC is creating a ten year plan for Fisher management.

Bears: What would Bear Lake be without bears? Bear tracks around the cottages in the snow are common; but there have been few sightings of them when most residents are around in the summer. One was spotted crossing Bear Lake Road in front of the Szumigala cottage in 2013, and more recently in 2015, Kay Johnston spotted one just past the tennis court going west and several were seen in 2016. Many long-time residents have never seen a live bear at the lake.

Bear Crosses Bear Lake Road

County Water Quality Task Force: WQTF meetings have been attended by Ken Balling, Roger Britz, Sean Redden and Bernie

Klaich representing the Association. Usually most of the agenda focuses on Chautauqua Lake, but occasionally some topics that may impact Bear Lake are discussed. Among them, Klaich reported in 2012 that septic system inspection for all of Chautauqua County looked like it would be implemented in the upcoming year (or later). *"No doubt this will be a big cost driver for homeowners, but a way to improve the quality of all watersheds"* said Klaich. At a Water Quality Task Force meeting on May 1, 2013, it was reported that the last time the County did an update to the septic system plan was in 1965. Septic system inspections could be random, but mandatory ones are required at time of sale of a property. In the Spring of 2015, the press reported that the Health Department had passed a regulation that all septic systems within two hundred fifty feet of county lakes that are over thirty years old would have to pass inspection. Beginning in 2015, the Health Department informed Bear Lake residents that all septic systems would be reviewed, starting with those within fifty feet of the water. While the focus seems to be on Chautauqua Lake, Klaich reported *"there will be a trickle down to the rest of the county as well. There has been an amnesty period, but enforcement is upcoming."* To date, many Bear Lake septic systems have already been replaced, and others are in process.

There has been much concern at the County level about the new invasive weeds, the Water Chestnuts and Hydrilla. Photos show a couple of Canadian geese with water chestnuts stuck in their feathers-- a new twist to the spread of invasive weeds; and there is no real fix to contain this spread by geese. None in Bear Lake yet!

Hydraulic Fracking: In 2015 a moratorium was put in place to prohibit fracking in New York State. Hopefully, this will continue, and Bear Lake will not be threatened with closure because of fracking as many fracked lakes in Pennsylvania have been.

CHAPTER 18
INVASIVE WEED CONTROL AT BEAR LAKE: A SUCCESS STORY

I n a letter to the Board of Directors of the Bear Lake Property
Owners Association of June 30, 1968, David Dorman, president, lamented that *"At nearly every meeting of the Association
since 1960, the problem of underwater weeds has been discussed with nearly everyone in attendance agreeing that
something should be done but undecided what to do."* This
chapter will detail the Association's efforts to control weeds
and the introduction and success of the Biocontrol Program
begun in 2010

The first mention of chemical treatment of weeds with
Ortho Diquat appeared in the minutes of a Board Meeting on
November 2, 1967, and there are weed permits and applications
secured by Arden Berndt from then until 1982 in the archives.
Permits were required because the chemical kills fish by lowering the oxygen levels, and only small areas could be treated,
such as beach and dock areas. At first, Fred Carr had the license
to apply the chemical courses after he and Dave Dorman took
a series of weed treatment courses at Jamestown Community
College. Getting the permit to treat the weeds took two and a
half weeks. The weeds were generally treated the first week in
June, and the cost for the eighteen gallons of Ortho Diquat was
twenty-eight dollars per gallon. The costs to property owners
was ten dollars each.

In the spring of 1968 the Association applied for and
received a permit to apply herbicide to eighteen acres of the

lake, consisting of an area two hundred feet wide along the north and east shorelines. The herbicide was applied on June 17, 1968; the lake was posted for no swimming for ten days after; and it cost about five hundred dollars for the area treated, which necessitated a special fund raising campaign for contributions. There was discussion of a donation being made based on lake frontage "as some people would benefit more than others," and there was also discussion of putting a box at Masiker's store for non-residents, such as fishermen, using the Lake to make donations. Initially, Chautauqua County paid about seventy-five percent (i.e., four hundred dollars) of the total cost of five hundred twenty-five dollars for treating the weeds; and residents would make up the difference.

There are yearly agreements between the BLPOA and the County representing the reimbursement process. Arden Berndt reported at the July 26, 1969 Annual Meeting that at Chautauqua Lake they have a budget of fifty-four thousand dollars of which five percent is reimbursed by the County. They use seven hundred to eight hundred gallons of herbicide, and *"they don't get as good control as we do. They raise funds by house-to-house contributions."* Diquat was used from 1968 to 1986 after which, Aquathol K was used until chemical treatment ceased. It became increasingly difficult to find someone to take the required herbicidal weed treatment course, and the Department of Environmental Conservation (DEC) had so narrowed the scope of chemical treatment—only along the Bear Lake Road shoreline and in the north end cove—that the decision to not have someone take the treatment course became inevitable. Of course, the invasive weed population—particularly of Eurasian Milfoil—exploded without chemical treatment. At times the lake looked more like a meadow than a lake. Something had to be done, and a weed committee was suggested and constituted at the 2007 Annual Meeting.

The Weed Committee was composed of Ken Balling (one of the former chemical treatment appliers), Bill Bennett,

Roger Britz, Anne Deming (chairperson), Bob Deming, Judy McQueary, Sean Redden, Dick Schulte, Marsha Sullivan and Ruth Szumigala. It met for the first time on July 20, 2007. The Agenda included updates on a meeting between Legislator Brian Abram and Anne Deming about applying for bed tax revenue, possible rental of the Cassadaga Lake harvester, the designation of Ken Balling and Sean Redden (with Roger Britz as alternate) as Bear Lake representatives on the county's Water Quality Task Force so that we would be party to any County planning about water issues. Anne Deming drafted and distributed a two page "draft copy" of "The Bear Lake Weed Control Plan," which was to be used for grant and bed tax funding. It set out the Weed Committee's mission, goals, and action plans for the first to fifth years and a proposed budget for 2008. Amended and approved, the plan was sent to the Board, the Supervisors of the Towns of Pomfret and Stockton and County legislator Brian Abram.

Weed Harvesting: As a result of the resolution at the July 2007 Annual Meeting, President Kris Wittmeyer was authorized to contact Tom Cooper (Cassadaga Lakes Association President) to rent the Cassadaga Lake weed harvester to cut weeds at Bear Lake. The harvester arrived for its first cut at 6:30 a.m. on July 30th, was met by Ken Balling and Bob Deming, and was given the four sites for weed harvesting: 1. in front of the Conservation Club and in both channels; 2. the north west bay and the "meadow" of weeds that had formed there. 3. another day of cutting the weeds in the "meadow"; and 4. the cutting of a path down the lake outside the docks, along the length of the lake. The harvester was docked at Jim Meder's dock at Muskie Point and also at Bill Ehmke's dock on the northwest end, and the harvested weeds were taken by tractor to the O'Brien farm on Kelly Hill Road. All told, the harvester was present for four days, and removed nineteen loads of weeds, at a cost to the Association of two thousand five hundred dollars.

At the Weed Committee's meeting on August 24, 2007 an evaluation of the harvesting reported that most residents were very pleased with the results. The agenda also included the approval of a Bed Tax application which Anne Deming had written, suggestions for other sources of funding, and a report from the BLPOA's representatives on the Water Quality Task Force Committee. At that meeting, the Weed Committee also decided to change its name to the Water Quality/Lake Management Committee so as to include periodic water quality testing not just weed control. Weed harvesting for 2008 was discussed at length. Some people didn't want it because too many weeds were not retrieved by the harvester and floating weeds interfered with boating. The Committee eventually recommended harvesting for a second year but requested that residents help clear up the floating weeds around their docks. The Bed Tax application was approved and plans for a New York State grant which Anne Deming would apply for were discussed.

The "Meadow"

157

Harvester cuts through the "Meadow"

During the winter of 2007 and spring of 2008, Anne Deming applied for and the Association was granted a $9,000 Member Initiative Grant from New York State Senator Catherine Young. The state grant (Legislative Aid Grant Contract #TM 08003) included funding for a second weed harvesting by the Cassadaga Lake harvester, for a lake mower to be towed behind a boat to work in close to docks, for two additional hand-held weed cutters to supplement the one purchased earlier, and for two long, hand-held rakes to use to gather the cut weeds. To ensure that the Board would not be liable when residents made use of the equipment, Deming requested the services of an attorney friend who prepared Hold Harmless Liability Forms to be signed by the residents before using the equipment, thereby absolving the Board of liability.

Lake Management: At its July 26, 2008, the Water Quality/ Lake Management Committee welcomed Deb Lanni and Chuck Haenel as new members. Reports on the status of weed harvesting, the state grant, the proposed status of incorporation as a 501©3 organization so that the Association would be eligible for charitable contributions, equipment purchases, and water quality testing were given. The Committee decided to simplify its name to the Lake Management Committee (LMC) and to fold itself into the Board as a Board committee, rather than remain an ad-hoc committee of the Board. At the same time, the earlier "Bear Lake Weed Control Plan" became the "Bear Lake Management Plan."

Other events began to propel the BLPOA towards a different mode of weed control. On August 23, 2008, Anne invited Jane Conroe, a Cleveland friend and an environmentalist from the Chautauqua Lake Association, to discuss weed control with the LMC and the Board. Following the meeting, the Demings took her out in their boat so that she could take "a grab sample" (a handful of weeds) from the lake to send to Dr. Robert L. Johnson, a Cornell University environmental scientist, who had been assisting the Chautauqua Lake Association with native herbivore applications (caddis flies, moths, and weevils) to control their invasive weeds, in other words, "natural" bio controls. In an October 6th email, Johnson reported that from Conroe's grab sample, it was evident that damage had indeed been done to the apical (i.e., top) stems of the Eurasian milfoil by the indigenous weevils native to Bear Lake. There were eight total weevils on the fifteen apical stems submitted, leading Johnson to report that *"there appears to be a large number of insects damaging milfoil and the milfoil showed it."* This very good news for Bear Lake offered a radical change in the weed control practices from chemical or harvesting to natural bio control.

Anne and Bob Deming, both associated with the SUNY Fredonia, decided to meet with Biology professor Dr. Tim Strakosh, and later with his class in environmental aquatic biology to ask for their help in developing a comprehensive management plan for Bear Lake. Such a plan would be necessary in order to get additional grants to support weed control, but the cost of about fifty thousand dollars would be prohibitive for the Association. The class and Professor Timothy Strakosh offered to do it for free. Based on examining the existing Lake

Management Plan, and adding scientific information about the quantity of weevils in the lake, they would ascertain the probability of using them for control of invasive Eurasian milfoil in Bear Lake. A fall semester end date for the plan was extended to a spring semester end date for the report of the students' research findings on Bear Lake.

When Strakosh left the College that spring, one of the students, Jen Rinehart, in the Fall class who at the time was enrolled in an Independent Study program with him, volunteered to pull together all of the students' findings into a comprehensive Lake Management Plan for Bear Lake. Incomplete at the end of that semester, Rinehart promised to but did not finish the report by May 13th. To finally get its management plan, the Association agreed to pay her ten dollars an hour to continue her work on the plan after graduation. Eventually, she delivered a ninety-six page report, but without any faculty review, it contained grammatical and some questionable scientific findings. The Association was unable to get a revised and usable Lake Management Plan and an Executive Summary from Rinehart that could be used for grant applications. In the fall of 2010, Rinehart did submit *Bear Lake Management Plan 2010,* a short summary of the samplings of weeds by the Johnson team at four GPS locations (A, B, C and D) and records of samples of milfoil/weevils at those sites sampled on June 17th, July 16th and August 12th of 2010 by the Johnson team. Pleased with the Johnson results, the Association agreed to contract with Dr. Johnson to place three thousand weevils into Bear Lake on August 24, 2010 to supplement the indigenous weevils already there, thus beginning a bio control plan to control the invasive Eurasian milfoil.

Using the Demings' boat, Board members, Anne and Bob Deming, with help from Roger Britz, Bernie Klaich, and later, Sid Potmesil, helped Johnson gather Eurasian milfoil samples at the four Johnson designated GPS sites twice each summer over the next four summers (2011-2014) to assess the effectiveness of the added weevils. [Locations of the Watermilfoil Herbivore sampling locations are on a map found in Maps section of Appendix C.] In 2015, a single sampling was collected from the now three test sites, there no longer being any milfoil in one of the sites. More sampling was not needed because the weevils had done an excellent job and the invasive weeds there were now well controlled.

Board members helping Johnson always learned something new when he was on the lake. He taught them, for example, *"that the weevils continuously move along the lake, laying two eggs on each milfoil tip to help assure their survival. If the milfoil tips are pink, the milfoil is healthy; if burgundy in color, there is damage to the tips, done by the weevils."* They also learned that Bear Lake did not have as bad a weed problem as many other lakes because our bio control program was working and was a much better treatment than cutting the weeds which only encouraged regrowth.

The first report about the "success" of the increased weevil population and milfoil demise was contained in a brief report from Dr. Johnson based on a comparison of the fall 2010 samplings and the July 2011 samplings. The 2010 sampling results following the August 24 weevil addition were quite encouraging: weevils predators per stem at Location B had a very high population. They had survived and increased. By July 2011, there was a much lower population of weevils, because there was very limited milfoil growth at Location B in 2011, which meant the weevils had done their good work there and moved on to other areas in the lake to eat the milfoil. Johnson remarked in his report that *"the important observation this year [2011] is that the water-milfoil plants were damaged at least as much as last year and their total growth appeared to be less."* He concluded that adding more weevils in 2011 would not be necessary, suggesting, however, that moths, another natural, indigenous predator, might be added in June of 2012 to further control the milfoil.

Dr. Bob Johnson on boat sampling Milfoil

Dr. Bob Johnson examining Milfoil stems with microscope

In August of 2012, Johnson reported the 2012 screening results of the Eurasian Watermilfoil sampled at Bear Lake by Racine-Johnson Aquatic Ecologists [he had by then retired from Cornell and established his own consulting firm of that name], and contrasted the 2012 results with the reported 2010 and 2011 weevil populations. In Bear Lake, only the aquatic weevil *Euhrychiopsis lecontei* is found, but two aquatic moth

(*Acentria ephemerella*) larvae were also found in that year's samples. Populations of the aquatic weevil change through the summer season and from year to year depending primarily on the quantity of milfoil available, overwintering conditions prior to the summer season, and on the amount of predation by pan fish. Johnson's summary concluded that the weevil population was enough to keep the milfoil growth relatively stable as long as they remained at current levels. Johnson recommended an increase in herbivore populations by augmenting with either aquatic weevils or moths for more milfoil control. The decision would be made before next summer about whether to add those insects. DEC permits needed to be in place, which he would secure. An electronic copy of Johnson's complete report (including tables and pictures) is available in the Bear Lake Association Archives. For more information on the two insect herbivores, see http://www.invasive.org/biocontrol/6Eurasian-Milfoil.html.

Dr. Johnson was back at Bear Lake in June 2013 to check on the status of the Eurasian Watermilfoil, collect the usual milfoil samples, and assess how soon to place moth larvae into the lake, which the Association had agreed would be the next phase of the weed bio control. *"Moths should be added at the same life stage as they appear in the Lake,"* Johnson recommended. *"Adding [moths] at the time of natural moth peak helps with better reproduction this year and hope for increases in natural lake moth production next year."* He planned to add moths through September because they start to overwinter in October.

Johnson returned to Bear Lake on July 5, 2013 to collect the usual 25 packets of milfoil stems from each of the usual three sites. Each foot-long milfoil stem collected was to be analyzed to determine the stage of the weevils and milfoil and the location and a rough estimate of the optimal time to augment moths in the lake. It appeared the moths and weevils were maturing late that year; in Chautauqua Lake, he noted, they were about two weeks late, hence the abundance of milfoil there and in Bear Lake that summer.

In his second report of July 12, 2013, Johnson reported that his analysis found very high levels of weevil damage at all three locations. He said *"You should see a lot of future damage as eggs are just hatching, and there are a lot of small larvae. This is the most adult weevils we have seen from a sampling; and they will continue laying more eggs now that should also hatch in a few weeks. There should be a lot of future damage as they appear to be just getting started. So looks very good."*.

Moths Added: Johnson planned to add moths after the weevils finished the major damage so that the moths would have some good food from plant re-growth to over-winter in. He did not think we needed to augment weevil herbivores again unless milfoil density increased greatly. He set up an aquatic moth (*Accentria*) augmention test and evaluation site on September 8, 2013, at a site in the north end of the Lake. Assisted by Roger Britz and Anne and Bob Deming, he deposited thirty small burlap bundles of various stages of moth development attached to an apical stem of Milfoil. He also brought some samples of moths in different developmental stages which he demonstrated for the "gatherers" with a microscope. *"It was exciting to actually see the microscopic critters under the microscope, and it is now our hope that this moth augmentation will complete Bear Lake's bio control plan begun in 2010"* said President Deming.

In December, Johnson delivered to the Board copies of his comprehensive report *Insect Herbivore Monitoring in Bear Lake from 2011 through 2013*. The one page Executive Summary of this report brought all good news: *"The main plot locations, A, B and D show a steady mean weevil population over the three years suggesting a stable reliable control of Watermilfoil growth in Bear Lake in the near term. An assessment of moth augmentation in the short term will likely continue in addition to ongoing documentation of weevil populations."* A copy of the Executive Summary of the report was made available with the complete report in the Association Archives.

Johnson's microscopic analysis of Watermilfoil apical tips collected by him, Anne and Bob Deming from the three locations on July 20, 2014 evidenced significant successes: *"the feeding on Watermilfoil by insects and in this case primarily by the weevil, has negatively influenced the aggressive growth of Eurasian Watermilfoil observed in Bear Lake during 2014.* A moth sampling was also conducted in the summer of 2015.

Bob Johnson's report, *Eurasian Watermilfoil's Insect Herbivores in Bear Lake from 2010 through 2014,* received in early May, 2015 was again full of good news. Since the addition of 3000 indigenous weevils in 2010, the aquatic weevil, *Euhrychiopsis lecontei,* had remained at a medium density feeding on the Milfoil. Johnson reported Bear Lake has a "robust" population of them with *the "highest densities of weevils per apical stem in the range of 1.5 to 3+ causing significant damage to watermilfoil."* At those densities, *"watermilfoil expansion is halted and often declines"* as it did in one of the three test sites on Bear Lake, and *the "steady weevil population over the last three years suggests a stable, reliable control of watermilfoil growth which will limit the growth of Eurasian watermilfoil into the future."* The indigenous, aquatic moth, *Acengtria ephemerella,* was also found in Bear Lake but at very low densities which prompted the addition of more of them in the summer of 2013. To date, that addition has not shown a marked increase in Milfoil destruction by moths.

Johnson concluded his report with these observations and recommendations for the future of the control program: *"There is always a possibility of a future year when control of watermilfoil may be less than desired but that should be the exception with good control returning the following year. Future planning should include consideration of increasing the efficiency of the herbivore activity on watermilfoil by encouraging future herbivore population increases by increasing predation on panfish*

*in the lake. The negative effect of sunfish feeding on the herbi-
vores is well documented. Preventing even a small amount of
this heavy feeding on them would likely allow for an increase in
weevils and moths feeding on Eurasian Milfoil. Therefore any
legal means to increase the populations of game fish in the lake
should be encouraged and pursued."* It should be noted that
Amish fishermen remove some of these panfish each year.

Grants: State, County and Town grants have funded most
of the Association's weed control efforts. Dr. Anne Deming
secured the first nine thousand dollar state grant in 2007. A
County Bed Tax grant of four thousand dollar grant which she
secured to monitor water quality and weed control was awarded
in 2011. Bed Tax Grant applications for four thousand dollars and five thousand dollars, prepared by Presidents Haenel
and Deming, were successful in two of the three subsequent
years with two additional extensions of these grants approved
through 2015. A one hundred thousand dollar grant, the largest
ever received, was granted by the State in 2015 to be used for
weed control and dredging. That grant, administered by the
Chautauqua County Department of Soil and Water is being
used to develop a new Bear Lake Management Plan and for
boat monitoring at the launch site. The possible dredging of
the Clever/Masiker channels, and the creek sandbar at Muskie
Point is being considered.

Yearly contributions from Chautauqua County and the
Towns of Pomfret and Stockton supplemented these grants in
most years. Deming's appeals to the county to increase the
annual allocation to control invasive weeds in the lake provided
the Association one thousand five hundred dollars beginning
in 2014, up from seven hundred fifty dollars in 2013 and five
hundred dollars annually before that. She expressed appreciation for the help of Legislators Brian Abram, John Runkle
and George Borrello and County Watershed Coordinators, Jeff
Diers and Dave McCoy, for their support in these efforts.

The bio control program begun in 2010 continues today. Bear Lake is the only one among the four Chautauqua County lakes and Lake Erie which uses bio control exclusively to control invasive weeds. It has proven to be very successful, affording good weed control and few toxic algae blooms.

CHAPTER 19
CAMP-IN-THE-WOODS/
THE "Y" CAMP

The "Y" Camp on the "other side" of the lake was an important part of Bear Lake for years. Many children from the "roadside" of the lake attended the camp. Former "roadside" campers Dorothy Dobbins, Ken Klocek, John Pierce, Richard Wang, Pat Petsch, Ruth Szumigala, and Roger Britz contributed to this chapter.

The camp began in 1928 when Clifford Pierce, state YMCA Secretary of Kansas and a native of Stockton, established a YMCA/YWCA camp next to his own Bear Lake campground, "Pierce Acres." Called the Camp-in-the-Woods or the "Y" Camp, Pierce gave it free to the Chautauqua County YMCA. The non-profit, non-denominational camp was intended to continue for twenty-eight years but eventually continued for forty-seven years, until the County Health Department forced its closing in 1975 because an adequate septic system for its increasing number of campers was not possible.

Harold S. Duncan, the County "Y" Secretary, appointed A. Warren Dayton, known as "the Admiral," as the first Director of the Camp which numbered two hundred fifty campers in its peak years. Dayton was also the principal at the Alexander Central School near Batavia. Later Earl Brooker, a Science Teacher and Assistant Principal at Brocton High School, and then Eugene Howard served as early Camp Directors.

According to former campers, *"boys went to Camp in July and girls in August, for a week to a month. They lived in two rows of twelve to fourteen Navy surplus tents erected on platforms, each tent sleeping eight. The tents were near the road leading into the Camp, arranged in a parabolic form. Campers slept on surplus Army cots, not bunk beds, one on either side of the entrance, two each on the other three sides. Campers were told not to touch the tent canvas, and, of course, they touched it, and the canvas leaked. The tents started near the mess hall, went past the pump, and down toward the road that came into the Camp from Route 380.*

Pierce Acres postcard

A view of a Tent

A counselor in each tent kept count of the kids in their tent, and supervised swimming and life-saving. Campers had to do chores in each tent. You attended Camp from the time you were eight until you were sixteen. At fourteen, you became a Counselor, and at sixteen, you became a Senior Counselor.

There was a mess hall among the old beech trees with a flagpole out front. At one time, Viola Cummings was the cook; she also made coffee for the counselors every morning. There was a large campfire circle, called the 'Church' that was a gathering place down near the lake; and the same benches used for the campfires were those you sat on for meals. There was also a nurse [Ruth Howard] *in the dispensary in the Red Shack on the top of the bank, which also served as the Craft Shack. After lunch, the Red Shack would open up so a camper could buy a candy bar as well as your craft stuff. The Pierce family campground was to the right (looking out at the lake) and the swamp was to the left of the mess hall and the tents.*

There was propane gas for cooking in the mess hall; in the late 1950s a totally new mess hall, across from 'The Palace' [the outhouse] *was built with a new kitchen. Water was pumped out of the lake, not out of a well. A tower was put up, and a reservoir was at the top of the tower. Although the pump was near the mess hall, they didn't often use it. The boys and girls brushed their teeth and bathed in the lake.*

Very near the swamp was an outhouse with four holes called 'The Palace.' It had fifty-five gallon cans underneath which were turned [i.e., emptied] *over into the swamp and were frequently cleaned by the campers as a form of punishment. In other words, you had about one hundred kids using this five by eight small "Palace" building."*

The Waterfront: A photo of the waterfront, labeled Pierce Acres, helps to identify what was there.

the Waterfront at Camp-in-the-Woods

The campers added that *"the dock was configured in typical Red Cross form. The shallow area nearest the land was called the 'Crib.' To go beyond the first dock, you had to pass 'the fifteen minutes test', which meant you had to tread water for ten to fifteen minutes in water over your head. To the left in the picture, there is a long ramp leading to a double diving board with what looks like a cage over it. That was for climbing up.*

Double diving board with climbing cage

172

Swinging tripod

Sometime later, a tripod swing was installed with rings that you could swing out from. The swing thing was tied to a tree that bent out over the shore, and there was an anchor back there that allowed you to swing forward on it. It was fairly close to shore. There was a little platform to stand on before swinging out. At one point Lefty [Eugene] Howard was the waterfront director.

In the inner shallow area was the 'Log'. You and a partner spun the log and walked along it. It had deep ridges on it, and moss growing on it. The purpose was to have fun and learn balance and cooperation with your partner." [One of the Pierce grandchildren recalls that *"that log was the same one my mother stood on.'*] *There was monitored swimming after breakfast for an hour—then activities like archery, twemty-two rifle target practice, baseball and other games played way back toward Route 380—a considerable walk!* [about a mile.]

When a camper went into the water, there was a board with little tags on it, and the camper moved the tag from one side of the board to the other side, indicating that you were in the water. Everyone in the water had a 'buddy;' and when the whistle blew you had to find your buddy and hold up her/his hand and your hand together.

There were six to eight canoes, some fitted with sails, which were kept on the right side of the dock. Once in a while, there would be a motor boat at the Camp; and the older campers learned to water ski behind it. There were bugle calls for everything. At reveille, you ran out of your tent and lined up. The first guy/girl in line had a taut rope; and everyone would stand behind him/her. Mess call was another bugle call as was taps. Sometimes, two buglers were used, one standing at the end of the dock, and the other standing up on the campground, repeating the notes to each other.

There were many traditions: the Hayride down Chautauqua Road to the Lamkin Bear Lake Store. At a certain time, there would be a swim across the lake, not a Red Cross requirement, with canoes (no row boats!) following the swimmers, and other forms of swimming activities. If you were caught doing something you weren't supposed to do, there was outhouse cleaning as a punishment [as mentioned above]. *Wednesday was visitors day and usually, lots of parents came to visit. Saturday night was for awards for swimming across the lake, doing something special like a back flip; these got you a scoop of ice cream. There were many, many mosquitos from the swamp. Occasionally someone came and sprayed, fogging, probably w ith DDT."*

Visitors day around the campfire

Ruth Wang Szumigala, a current Bear Lake resident, was eleven years old when she first went to Y Camp. She formerly stayed instead at the Pierce cottage, her grandfather's cottage. Dorothy Dobbins, also a current resident, started camp in 1936 when she was ten *"because my mother decided that since we were here for the summer, I needed friends to play with."* So she and her sister Marion went to camp until 1941 when they advanced to be counselors. Dorothy's three sons—Bob, Chuck and Jim—all went to camp beginning when they were ten. Eventually, Dorothy, who had her Junior and Senior Lifesaving Badges, was Sports Director, her cousin Marge Frisbee Suggs was Waterfront Director, and her college friend, Lois Ebling Pierce, was Arts and Crafts Director.

Ken Klocek went to camp in 1959, but only for one year since he and his brother went instead to Camp Merz, the Boy Scout Camp on Chautauqua Lake. He recalls that *"the Y Camp was tuned in to the Lake."* Once a week, there was an expedition to the Lamkin Store, but you had to be a swimmer to do it. He wasn't allowed to go, because he had not passed the requisite swimming level. The tie to the north side of the lake was the bugle: reveille at 8:00 a.m. and taps at sunset. The whole lake heard it.

Roger Britz started going to Camp in 1952 when he was eight. He remembers the Mess Hall being used as a rec hall and the Admiral's cabin being back in the woods [i.e., John Pierce's cabin discussed in Chapter 11]. Roger doesn't remember dumping the latrine barrels into the swamp but rather into the woods. *"There was skinny dipping with a bar of soap, and when you're a little kid, that was something of a shock,"* he explained. Like the ending of the Massiker/Clever Store, the ending of the Y Camp was memorable and is still missed by many current "Bear Lake side" dwellers and former campers.

175

CHAPTER 20
THE BASKET FACTORY ON BEAR LAKE ROAD

T he basket factory, the only commercial industry on Bear Lake Road in the1920s, was mentioned by longtime residents as being significant to Bear Lake history. So it is included here.

William Sloan and Mabel Azalia (Blodgett) Snell acquired land along Bear Lake Road for a basket factory from Emerson J. Turk and Eva Turk on September 12, 1921 according to a deed in the Chautauqua County Clerk's Office (*Deeds, Liber 471*, page 591). Sometime later, probably in the later 1920s, the Snell Family built the first of what would eventually become four buildings that formed a basket factory complex on the site where currently Cliff Couchman has his automobile restoration building. The Snell family lived in what the late Willie Snell called "the old home" on Sodom Road (also known as Turk Road, named for the Turk family who lived in that vicinity). Sodom Road ran between the Fredonia-Stockton Road and Kelly Hill Road, and remnants of the old road are still visible from the Fredonia-Stockton Road.

The Snells eventually sold the property and the basket factory to the co-partnership of Wallace Phillips Jr. of Gardenville, New York and Benjamin Klopp of Derby, New York on June 5, 1945, though not recorded until 8/28/45, for "one or more dollars," (again, according to the deed cited above). Wallace Phillips, in business with his brother William W. Phillips, already owned a basket factory in downtown

Buffalo, known as the Phillips Brothers Basket Factory, a name which was also given to the Bear Lake Road site.

A letter from Karen Phillips, the daughter-in-law of William W. Phillips, to a Michael Wicker at the Chautauqua Conservation Club in 2015 was turned over to the authors of this history for research and comment and led to new information about the factory. Phillips noted in that letter that William Phillips was the manager of the factory on Bear Lake Road and that the brothers, William and Wallace, also owned a veneer mill at the same site. Phillips also provided other, helpful information, about David Phillips, Wallace's son, and about Lewis T. Phillips *"who ran the veneer mill on Bear Lake."*

Additional information about the Phillips was received from Raymond Kelsey, who as a teenager worked at the basket factory from 1959 to 1960 before graduating from high school. Kelsey was referred by Helen Piersons, Town of Stockton Historian. In a telephone interview on August 26, 2015, he mentioned that the basket factory was run by David Phillips, son of Wallace Phillips. He also referred to an Obituary in the *Fredonia Censor* (8/9/1951) which stated that William W. Phillips, manager of the Phillips Brothers Basket Factory of Bear Lake, *"had died of a seizure the day before."* William Phillips had resided in Fredonia for nine and a half years, and had two brothers Wallace Phillips of Orchard Park and Lewis Phillips of Topeka, Kansas. Lewis T. Phillips Jr. had run the veneer mill in one of the basket factory's buildings. According to Kelsey *"he lived in a shack on the property and had a black and white TV on which we* [he and Kelsey] *sometimes watched Milton Berle."* Kelsey's mother, Margaret, also worked at the Basket Factory (making Picnic baskets) and his former wife, Mary Lou Carlson worked there making Easter Baskets where she *"once did five dozen baskets in one day"* (reputedly a record). According to Kelsey, there were as many as fifty people working there in spite of the "low wages." By the time he worked there, they were no longer making grape baskets, but were instead making a variety of other baskets—bread, Easter, and picnic baskets.

The basket factory consisted of a boiler room, which provided steam for a steam room and for two buildings where the employees worked. In the picture of the basket factory in an August 19, 1953 *Stockton Town Picnic* program, the boiler building is at the far left, with the smokestack. Originally, the building was farther up the hill, was called the "nailing shack or shed," and was where the basket factory apparently started. It was decided, however, that this building was too far away from the buildings near Bear Lake Road to easily move the stock. Consequently, the original building was eventually deserted and fell down. The buildings in the middle and on the right side of that same picture are said to have burned down. The current Couchman building, (not in the picture) was not built on the site until 1969.

PHILLIP'S BROS. BASKETS, Stockton, N. Y.
Bear Lake Road

The Bear Lake Basket Factory

During the time Kelsey worked there, there were two buildings, one near the road and another *"up the hill in the back. In the lower building, there was a dye room, where the basket material, called the 'veneer,' was dyed primarily for the Easter baskets, a lathe used to cut the wood pieces into veneer, sometimes as long as fifteen feet, a steam room where the veneer was soaked to bend it, and a general work room."* The entire basket factory operation was heated by radiators supplied with hot water by the boiler. The process went something like this: *"logs were delivered that were either cut to length or were cut to length at the basket factory; then the logs were put through the lathe which cut them into thin strips, called 'veneer,' which were then stacked high before being put through the clipper and cut into the different width sizes needed for the various baskets. The strips of veneer were then put into the steam room to bend them to the appropriate shape,"* said Kelsey.

Some of Kelsey's information repeats what Karen Phillips had said in her letter about the Phillips family. Wallace Phillips apparently took over the business when his brother William died; and his son, David, later became manager and owner. Kelsey recalled that Jack Kohl and Helen Kenny, both from Stockton, also worked as managers.

According to deeds in the Clerk's Office, the property "changed hands" on 9/27/77 from Phillips Brothers to Phillips Bros. Basket Co. In 1983, it apparently reverted to ownership by Chautauqua County, was then purchased by Ralph Phillips Sr on 12/21/84, and was finally sold to Clifford and Marie Couchman of 8166 Bear Lake road on 10/16/2000. One of the joys of living at Bear Lake, is seeing Cliff's old cars and trucks drive down the road. Although the basket factory, remembered by many residents, may be gone, cars from that era still remain here thanks to the Couchmans.

CHAPTER 21
DID YOU KNOW THAT?

T his chapter attempts to capture facts, legends, and myths about Bear Lake that residents have shared for generations. Following are some of them.

- Bear Lake was named when two boys, Harlow Crissey and Jason Silsby from Stockton encountered two bear cubs up a tree at a nearby lake. Harlow reputedly went home to get a gun, leaving Jason keeping watch over the cubs. Before Harlow's return, the mother bear called her two cubs down from the tree and disappeared with them into the bushes. According to Cathryn Berndt's *Stockton Seen Through the Rear View Mirror* (1987, 23), Jason's story about the bear cubs *"so amused the settlers that the Lake was nicknamed 'Bear Lake;' and the name stuck."*

- For the longest time, Leroy Pierce had the only phone line on Bear Lake. Later there were two, one for Walter Lamkin and one for Everett Alden. As late as the 1980s, there were as many as five parties on one line with the phones continuously busy.

- Early residents of Bear Lake went to the east end of the Lake to learn to swim, because the west end was too shallow.

- Bear Lake had a dump reserved for resident use that was managed by Walt Lamkin.

- The Masiker store, opened in 1962, was sold to Richard and Kay Orloff in 1979, to Art and Marlene Clever in 1981; and then sold back to Emery M Masiker in 2016.

The Masiker/Orloff/Clever/Masiker Store

- There was a community picnic ground at the Sahle Cottage, where the first Association Annual Meeting and Picnic was held. The location has moved around since then, from the Clever picnic pavillion to Bill Bennett's home on the canal, to Mogford's in the woods, to Wittmeyer's, to Haenel's, to Britz's, to Deming's, Latko's and to Potmesil's to date.

- The Pierce, 10 bedroom"hotel" was located in the middle of the Bear Lake Road that sold chicken dinners cooked by Minnie (Blodgett) Pierce, ice cream from the Pierce cold storage, and pies also baked by Mrs.Pierce. There was also an apple orchard with picnic tables on the Pierce property (where the Hagadorn cottage now stands).

- There was a basket factory at the west end of the Lake where Cliff Couchman now has his automobile restoration building, across the street was the I-Del-Ours [Idle Hours] cottage and the Bear Lake Turkey Farm owned by Herbert Reimann.

- There was a YMCA summer camp on Gravel Point on the south side of the lake, on the property owned by the Clifford Pierce family of Stockton; it operated from 1928 until 1975.

- The former Elizabeth Crocker cottage (once next door to the Reddens) was not, as rumor has it, *"moved across the ice one winter from Pierce Acres."* Rather, it was the Johnston's cottage, which had at first been an ice house at the Brocton rail yards, that was moved two more times, first to Pierce Acres, and finally across the frozen lake to become the boat livery for Walt Lamkin's general store across the street from it.

Lamkin's Boat Livery postcard

- The Lamkin store building was also rumored to have been moved across the frozen lake. Not moved across the lake, it was, however, once a garage up on the hill on the Lamkin property, was later moved to Bear Lake Road, remodeled as a general store, complete with a gas pump, and finally remodeled again to become the Martz Cottage.

- A relative of Lucille Ball's rented the Lamkin boat livery building, and Lucy herself stayed there when she was young.

- There is a song, "On the Lake," written about Bear Lake in the 1980s by Greg Birmingham which recounts many funny facts about Bear Lake at the time.

- Bear Lake is currently stocked by the DEC each year with Muskellunge, every other year with Walleye fingerlings, and with Brown Trout in the outlet every other year.

- Bear Lake is in both the Town of Stockton and the Town of Pomfret, the division occurring on a line crossing the lake running in a straight line down Bacheller Hill Road and across the lake to the former Y Camp.

- A Black Bear crossed in front of the Szumigala Cottage in the summer of 2013, an unusual summer visit for a bear; two cubs and another adult bear were sighted in the summer of 2015; and another one on Gilbert Drive in the spring of 2016. Bear footprints are often found around cottages in winter, but rarely in summer; and many residents have had their bird feeders vandalized by bears.

Black Bear crosses Szumigala's yard

- Bald Eagles and Fishers also called Fisher Cats (weasel-like mammals) have recently established habitats around the lake, joining the usual long-time residents, Canada Geese, Great Blue Herons, Beavers, and an occasional Mink.

- Since 2010, Bear Lake is the single lake of the five in Western New York, using only natural bio controls to control invasive Eurasian Milfoil.

- The shallower, northwest bay was called Cob Cove.

- The Frasier house (now the Martz house) built in 1941, was the first house built east of the Leroy L Pierce house after Pierce had some of his extensive property surveyed and sold in 1921, 1925 and later in 1945. The Case [now Mogford] and Bogner cottages were the first cottages built on that Pierce land.

- William ("Billy") and George Reimann, early Bear Lake residents, helped build the Panama Canal.

- The current Linde cottage on the east corner of Bear Lake Road and Lawrence Drive was originally called the "Pair-A-Dice" by its owners, Leona (known as "Le," of the Reimann family) and Lewis Traub. The Birminghams/Reimanns had other interesting names for their Bear Lake cottages: Fairview, Shady Rest, Idel-Ours.

- "Old Emery" Masiker (Emery A) built the two canals at the campground, and caught snapping turtles in the outlets for "turtle soup on Sundays;" he also made authentic-looking Indian arrowheads/points.

- The nearby village of Stockton was formerly called "Bear Creek Corners," "Delanti," and "Moons Station."

- The Bear Lake Property Owners Association Inc. Board changed its name to the Bear Lake Association Inc. and updated its mission in 2014, qualifying it to apply for 501©3 not-for-profit status. That status, granted in 2015, now allows it to raise tax advantaged funds from individuals, foundations, and corporations.

- A "Total Maximum Daily Load" (TMDL) plan for Bear Lake was completed by the New York State Department of Environmental Conservation, under mandate from the Federal Environmental Protection Agency in February 2015. Because Bear Lake was designated as an "impaired lake," it required septic system inspections, improvements, or replacements, which have since been or are currently being completed.

- In 1988, the Tennessee Gas Transmission Company, under a permit from the DEC, removed the beaver dams in the outlet, causing very low lake levels. Since then, adjoining property owners along the Bear Lake outlet with DEC permits remove the dams when the lake rises too high. Reputedly, within twenty-four hours, the beavers rebuild those dams.

- In 1990-91, the Association actively opposed a Town of Pomfret rezoning permit to build a recycling landfill on Bacheller Hill Road

- Honorary Board status for nine or more years of Board service was created in 2012 by the BLPOA and conferred to date upon Arden Berndt, Mary Ellen Dorsett, Dave Dorman, Don Hoch, Carl Loiocano and Anne Deming.

- There were once pet raccoons, pet ducks, a pet crow, and a pet pig in addition to pet cats and dogs on the lake.

- A Cassadaga Lake resident once regularly flew his sea plane from there to Bear Lake to visit a Bear Lake resident; sea planes still land on the lake from time to time.

- Tiny Bear Lake is, in fact, the "headwaters of the Mississippi," because you can actually navigate by canoe or kayak from Bear Lake to the Gulf of Mexico, with some portage involved of course. The route takes you from Bear Lake to Bear Lake Creek to Cassadaga Creek to Conewango Creek to the Allegheny and Monongahela Rivers to the Ohio River, on to the Mississippi River and into the Gulf of Mexico.

- There was a "Bear Lake Drive-In" at the corner of Bear Lake Road, Kelly Hill Road, and Bacheller Hill Road which offered ice cream, hot dogs and pizza.

- According to legend, an Indian princess is buried outside the former Basket Factory (now Cliff Couchman's car/truck restoration building); and a second Indian princess drowned in Bear Lake, after which her father put a curse on Bear Lake.

- The red house until recently located east of the former Clever/Masiker Store, is the second house on Bear Lake that was moved around the lake. Moved in two pieces down Bear Lake Road from where the Potmesil house now stands, it was moved again in 2016, to Springville. The Johnston cottage, cited above, was moved three times: from the Brocton rail yard to the Pierce property and then across the lake to its current location.

The red house is moved again!

- The lake has had a course for water skiers for many years; and reputedly, the former New York State Barefoot Ski Champion still lives on the lake.

- At least six current or retired volunteer firemen, four current or retired corrections/police officers, several former teachers, four retired professors, and at least three plumbers live at Bear Lake in 2017.

- Bear Lake has had an hotel, two general stores, three ice cream stands, a restaurant, Y camp, a basket factory, a turkey farm, a dump, and three boat liveries in its history.

- The two canals to the west of the former Masiker/Clever Store were initially dug by hand; and the bricks for the store were also handmade.

- Baskets were made, maple sugar gathered and sold, and bees, turkeys, and cattle raised around Bear Lake.

- A prominent fundraising firm run by an equally prominent Bear Lake resident had offices in New York City, San Francisco, and in little Stockton.

- Children from New York City spent summers through a "Sunshine Program" at the Leroy Pierce hotel/house.

- Bear Lake has its very own Weather Station and once had a car inspection station on Bachelller Hill Road.

Bear Lake Weather Station

- Bear Lake overflowed its banks in 1972, 1979, 2012 during Hurricane Sandy and the flood in July 2015; flooding prior to 1972 is unknown to the authors

Sean Deming rescues dock pieces for neighbors during the 1979 flood

A cottage surrounded by water after Hurricane Sandy in 2012

Clever campground flooded after the torrential downpour of July 2015

- Dr. Courtney Wigdahl-Perry of the SUNY Fredonia Biology Department and her undergraduate and graduate students are currently studying Bear Lake's water quality, aqua culture, and post-glacial history.

Dr. Wigdahl-Perry and her students get ready to study Bear Lake

- The two women in the very large, 1939, Bear Lake photo at Cabela's in Cheektowaga are Marguerite Dickens Perkins and Ruth Ray. Marguerite stayed in Martha Wiser's house when her parents, Homer and Elma Perkins, lived in that cottage that they built; and the two women really caught those large Muskies in Bear Lake.

Marguerite Dickens (Perkins) of the Perkins family and Ruth Ray caught huge muskies in 1939 in Bear Lake

APPENDIX A
BEAR LAKE PROPERTY OWNERS ASSOCIATION AND THE BEAR LAKE ASSOCIATION INCORPORATORS, OFFICERS AND DIRECTORS (1949-2017)

Incorporators

1949: Walter W. Lamkin, John Rawson, Luther L. Pierce, Orval Brior, Hattie Sahle

Officers & Directors

1949: President, Hallie Sahle; Vice President, Walter Lamkin; Secretary, Lena Brior; Treasurer, Burnadette Gilbert

1950: [elected at the First Annual Meeting]; President, Raymond Frasier; Vice President, John Rawson; Secretary, Lena Brior; Treasurer, Burnadette Gibert; Directors: Andrew Elliott, Edward Gilson

1951: President, Raymond Frasier; Vice President, John Rawson; Secretary, Lena Brior; Treasurer, Burnadette Gilbert; Directors: Walter Lamkin, Luther Pierce

1952: President, Raymond Frasier; Vice President, John Rawson; Secretary, Jane Sahle; Treasurer, Burnadette Gilbert; Directors: Edwin Case, Albert Wolfe

1953: President, Raymond Frasier; Vice President, John Rawson; Secretary, Elizabeth Crocker; Treasurer, Agatha Case; Director: Hattie Sahle

1954: President, Raymond Frasier; Vice President, John Rawson; Secretary, Elizabeth Crocker; Treasurer, Agatha Case; Directors: Edward Gilson, Andrew Elliott

1955: President, Raymond Frasier; Vice President, John Rawson; Secretary, Elizabeth Crocker; Treasurer, Agatha Case; Directors: William Hartman, John Sahle

1956: [no record of the Annual Meeting or Board Meetings was found.]

1957: President, John Rawson; Vice President, Arden Berndt; Secretary, Elizabeth Crocker; Treasurer, Agatha Case; Directors: Donald Hoch, Ray Frasier, William Hartman, John Sahle, and [?] Cleveland

1958: same Officers and Directors as 1957, elected by acclamation of members; new Directors: Gerald Lawrence, John Harkness

1959: President, Arden Berndt; Vice President, Raymond Frasier; Secretary, Elizabeth Crocker; Treasurer, Agatha Case; Directors: [?] Cleveland, Frances DeLand, Don Hoch, Gerald Lawrence, John Harkness

1960: same Officers as 1959; Directors: Mrs. Elton Hall

1961: President, Raymond Frasier; Vice President, Arden Berndt; Secretary, Elizabeth Crocker; Treasurer, Agatha Case; Directors: Mrs Roy Nelson, Robert Purcell

1962: same Officers; new Director: Richard Birmingham

1963: [no meeting held in 1963]

1964: President, Nancy Schifferli; Vice President, Donald Hoch; Secretary, Elizabeth Crocker; Treasurer, Mrs. David Dorman; Directors: Elton Hall, James Johnson

1965: President, David Dorman; Vice President, Nancy Schifferli; Secretary, Elizabeth Crocker; Treasurer, Donald Pierson; Directors: Mrs. Betts, Arden Berndt

1966: President, David Dorman; Vice President, Paul Cave; Secretary, Elizabeth Crocker; Treasurer, Donald Pierson; Directors: Mrs. William McClelland, Lewis Crocker

1967: [no record of meetings found]

1968: President, David Dorman; Vice President, Elton Hall; Secretary, Shirley Thorp; Treasurer, Helen Carr; Directors: William McClelland, Woody Hart, John Harkness, Arden Berndt, Art Clever, W. E. Betts

1969: President, David Dorman; Vice President, Elton Hall; Secretary, Shirley Thorp; Treasurer, Mary Ellen Dorset, Directors: Fred Carr replaced William McClelland; Muriel Alden replaced Woody Hart

1970: [same Officers]

1971: [same Officers]; LeRoy Goldhardt replaced Muriel Alden; new Directors: John Harkness, Arden Berndt, Richard Birmingham

1972: [same Officers and Directors]

1973–1974: [no record of meetings found]

1975: [no record of Officers] Directors: LeRoy Goldhardt, Herbert Bogner, Dick Wolf replaced Morris Clawson (YMCA), Muriel Alden

1976: [no record of meetings found]

1977: President, David Dorman; Vice President, Arden Berndt; Secretary, Mary Ellen Dorset; Treasurer, Fred Carr; Directors: Richard Birmingham, Herbert Bogner, LeRoy Goldhardt, Dick Wolf, John Harkness

1978–1979: [no record of meetings found]

1980: President, Arden Berndt; Secretary, Robert Deming, Directors: LeRoy Goldhardt, Dorothy Steff, Velma Masiker, Walter Hornburg, Elmer Carlson, Ann Berndt, Richard Birmingham, Walter Schultz (Conservation Club)

1981: President, Richard Birmingham; Vice President, Chuck Johnston; Secretary, Robert Deming; Treasurer, Velma Masiker; Directors: Walter Hornburg, Elmer Carlson, Don Hoch, Carl Loiocano, Helen Carr, LeRoy Goldhardt, Ann Berndt, Dorothy Steff

1982: [no record of meetings found]

1983: President, Don Hoch; Vice President, Carl Loiocano; Secretary, Dorothy Dobbins; Treasurer, Helen Carr; Directors: Stan Tabasco, Dave Hosler, Cliff Couchman, Chuck Johnston, Brad Sullivan, Walter Schultz (Conservation Club)

1984: President, Don Hoch; Vice President, Carl Loiocano; Secretary, Velma Masiker (resigned and replaced by Jean Loiocano); Treasurer, Helen Carr; new Directors: Dave Couchman, Brad Sullivan

1985: President, Don Hoch; Vice President, Carl Loiocano; Secretary, Kay Orloff; Treasurer, Davd Couchman; new Director: Bud Willey

1986: [no record of meetings found]

1987: President, Don Hoch; Vice President, Carl Loiocano; Secretary, Mary Ann Balling; Treasurer, Dave Couchman; Directors: Stan Tabasco, Deb Lanni, Bud Willey.

1988: [same Officers and Directors]; new Director: Tom Hughes.

1989: [no record of meetings found]

1990: [same Officers and Directors as in 1987 and 1988; new Director: Walter Schultz (Conservation Club)]

1991: President, Don Hoch; Vice President, Carl Loiocano; Second Vice President, Cliff Couchman; Secretary, Mary Ann Balling; Treasurer, Dave Couchman; Directors: Bud Willey, Stan Tabasco, Deb Lanni, Tom Hughes, Bill Bennett, Walter Schultz (Conservation Club)

1992: [no record of meetings found]

1993: [same Officers and Board of Directors as 1991]

1994: President, Cliff Couchman; Vice President, Tom Hughes; Secretary, Deb Lanni; Treasurer, Dave Couchman; Directors: Dave Reis, Bill Bennett, Bud Willey, Stan Tabasco, Don Hoch, Walter Schultz (Conservation Club)

1995: [no record of meetings found[

1996: [same Officers and Board of Directors as 1994]

1997–2002: [no records of meetings found; Cliff Couchman was President during this period]

2003: President, Kris Wittmeyer; Secretary, Cathye Mogford; Treasurer, Dave Couchman; [no record of Directors found].

2004–2005: President, Kris Wittmeyer; Secretary, Cathye Mogford; Treasurer, Dave Couchman; [no record of Directors found].

2006: President, Kris Wittmeyer; no Vice President; acting Treasurer, Kris Wittmeyer; Secretary, Cathye Mogford; [no record of Directors found].

2007: President, Kris Wittmeyer; Vice President, Richard Schulte; Secretary, Cathye Mogford; Treasurer, Marie Couchman; Directors: Anne Deming, Stan Tabasco, Carl Loiocano, Don Hoch, Dana Rifogiato, Dave Couchman, Cliff Couchman, Bill Bennett

2008–2009: [no record of meetings found]

2010: President, Chuck Haenel; Vice President, Dick Schulte; Secretary, Deb Lanni; Treasurer, Cindy Britz; Directors: Anne Deming, Jessie Green, Roger Britz, Stan Tabasco, Sean Redden, Bernie Klaich (Conservation Club), Pat Syracuse, Don Kobel, Bob Deming

2011: [Dick Schulte, President; same Board of Directors as 2010]

2011: President, Anne Deming replaced Dick Schulte who resigned mid-term in 2011); Vice President, Chuck Haenel; Secretary, Jessie Green; Treasurer, Cindy Britz; Directors: Roger Britz, Bob Deming, Don Kobel, Deb Lanni, Sean Redden, Dick Schulte, Pat Syracuse, Stan Tabasco, Tim Rommel, Sid Potmesil, Bernie Klaich (Conservation Club)

2012: [same Officers and Directors]

2013: President, Anne Deming; First Vice President, Roger Britz; Second Vice President, Sid Potmesil; Secretary, Bob Deming; Treasurer, Cindy Britz; Directors: Jessie Green, Chuck Haenel, Don Kobel, Sean Redden, Tim Rommel, Pat Syracuse, Dick Schulte, Bernie Klaich (Consevation Club), Dave Stengel

2014: [same Officers and Directors, except Jessie Green who died and Mike Radomski who was new]

2015: President, Sid Potmesil; Vice President, Don Kobel; Secretary, Bob Deming; Treasurer, Pat Syracuse; Directors: Anne Deming, Cindy Britz, Roger Britz, Sean Redden, Tim Rommel, Dave Stengel, Brenda Hagadorn, Beth Latko, Mike Radomski

2016: [same Officers and Directors]

2017: President, Sid Potmesil; Vice President, Don Kobel; Secretary, Beth Latko; Treasurer, Pat Syracuse; Directors: Sean Redden, Tim Rommel, Dave Stengel, Brenda Hagadorn, Bob Deming; new Director, Steve Latko

APPENDIX B
THE EARLY LANDOWNERS AROUND BEAR LAKE

This Appendix about early landowners is dense, one might say "obtuse," but helpful we hope to understanding the early patterns of land ownership around Bear Lake and the links to families discussed in chapters 3-12.

The digitized copy of a Holland Land Company map is from a map book kept by the HLC agent to mark lots as they were sold. From about 1836, it was supplied by Michelle Henry, Chautauqua County Historian, who in a 2015 email accompanying the map said that *"the original is in a large bound volume of maps* [organized] *by town/range that was used by the Holland Land Company to mark lots sold/contracted. It is not dated but contains references to contracts that pre-date 1836. It is not a copy* [i.e., it is the orginal], *and contains references (I think) to the field notebooks in our* [the Chautauqua County Clerk's] *collection. The numbers 18-424 on the Chauncey Warren property, for example, indicate a volume and page of survey field notes, written by the original surveyors, describing the lot."* Some of the original survey field notebooks are available at several places/libraries in Chautauqua County. They contain very useful physical descriptions of the lots and their measurements in links and chains as described in Chapter 2. Other resources used to trace early landowners include additional maps: a wall map from 1854 supplied by Helen Piersons, Town of Stockton Historian; the 1867 Chautauqua County Atlas; the 1881 Chautauqua County Atlas (available online);

and a 1916 map of Chautauqua County. Copies of these maps can be found in Appendix C.

Surprisingly, there were only three purchases of Lots from the Holland Land Company through 1810. According to the compilation made by Virginia Washburn Barden in her *Holland Land Company Earliest Sales in Chautauqua County New York*, these three purchases were: Lot #48 (Town of Stockton) by Dr. John Thompson on October 30, 1809 [no acreage given]; Lot #47 by Dr. John Thompson, October 30, 1809 (p. 69);[xii] and Lot #50 in the Town of Pomfret by Benjamin Barrett on May, 6 1809.[xiii] These early purchases were compiled from a single ledger for all surveyed townships kept by William Peacock in the Batavia Office of the Holland Land Company. Later, Peacock kept separate ledgers for each township.

Lots: We have organized the discussion of the settlement of the Bear Lake area around the relevant Lot numbers in the two towns of Stockton and Pomfret in which Bear Lake is located, starting with Lots # 56, 48 and 47 in the Town of Stockton.

LOT # 56: John P. Downs' *Chautauqua County and Its People* (1921)[xiv] notes there was a Justus Jones on Lot # 56 in September, 1830; and this information is also in Andrew Young's *History of Chautauqua County,*[xv] which notes some of the earliest landowners who purchased lots around the south and east sides of Bear Lake from the Holland Land Company in the early nineteenth century.

Lois Barris' *Holland Land Company Delinquent Contracts in Chautauqua County New York*[xvi] lists the following delinquent contract: Peleg Redfield, who took out his contract on September 3, 1810 for three hundred thirty-three acres was a "nonresident," according to a notation in the leather bound notebook generated by the field agent. Redfield's property is described as follows: *"dry, beach, maple on the east line; SW gentle rise; upland S; M swail NW black ash swamp; pretty good"* [Lot 56, Township 4, Range 12.][xvii]

The compilation of "delinquent contracts" like Redfields was made by a field agent who traveled the county on horseback, distributing notices to contract owners who were delinquent in their payments. He also described the properties. According to Barris' "Introduction," the delinquent contracts are found in two journals. The first journal (a double-page ledger) was organized chronologically by Lot, Town, and Range. It was probably compiled around 1829. The second journal, apparently written by the same agent, duplicates the information in the first journal without property descriptions but with names and dates of renewals. These renewals were from 1829 and early 1830.

The 1836 Holland Land Company map[xviii] notes that Chauncey Warren purchased two hundred seventy-three acres before 1836 (Chauncey Warren was the son of Calvin Warren who settled in Stockton in 1816 from Windham, Connecticut; Lucien Warren (no relation) also owned part of Lot 56 and part of Lot 47).[xix]

In the Piersons wall map of 1854, one J. Goodreck is also indicated as an owner of part of Lot #56. No owners are listed for the south side of Bear Lake in the 1867 Chautauqua County Atlas (even though there were landowners noted in an earlier map). In the 1881 Chautauqua County Atlas (available online), the owners of Lot #56 include: L.C. Warren, J. Webb Warren, and Mrs. A. K. Warren. No one is listed as owning Lot #56 in the 1916 map of Chautauqua County.

LOT #48: LOT #48 is on the eastern border of Bear Lake in the Town of Stockton. Its earliest landowner appears to be John Silsby (1809), also mentioned in John P. Downs' *Chautauqua County and Its People*; then Ebenezer Tyler (April, 1811) and Solomon Tyler (April, 1811).[xx] Downs also lists Aaron Jones as a purchaser of part of Lot #48 in May, 1815. Other landowners before 1836 include Nathan and Lamson Grovenor and Sylvannus Crissey.

The 1854 wall map also shows owners of Lot #48 as A.K. Warren, S. Crissey, J. Mitchell and C. Thompson; and the 1881 Chautauqua County Atlas lists owners of Lot #48 as J. E. Bachellor (one hundred ninety-nine acres), C. M. Williams (twenty-two acres), and J. Webb Warren (one hundred fifth-six acres). And, finally, the 1916 map of Chautauqua County lists the following as landowners of Lot #48: G. M. Wert (one hundred thirty-nine acres), CA30/St (twenty-eight acres), Kelly Bros (twenty acres), and a Kelly Saw Mill.

LOT # 47: LOT #47 includes the Bear Creek outlet to current Route 380 and south of that route parallel to current Bowen Road. Barris' *Delinquent Contracts*[xxi] notes that one Joseph Bailey was delinquent on fifty acres, part of Lot #47 on January 31, 1820. Records indicate that Alanson Bailey and widow Bailey were residents, that thirty acres had been improved; that there was a frame house and barn and thirty fruit trees. Notes on land conditions indicate that it was *"dry gravelly good lot for all kinds of grain and fruit,"* and that the Baileys would see to repaying the contract "soon," and, on May 27, 1830, Alanson Bailey renewed the contract.

Barris also summarizes that one Erastus Fox and Veniah Fox were delinquent on their seventy-one acres in the west part of Lot #47. Their contract was January 31, 1830. Veniah Fox was resident on the eastern part of Lot #47, and Erastus Fox was resident on the western part. Forty acres were improved at the time of the delinquent review; there was a log house and a frame house and a frame barn. There were also eighty fruit trees and the ground was *"dry gravelly, good lot for wheat and fruit."*[xxii]

Finally, Barris notes that Eli Webster had a delinquent contract on ninety-five acres on part of Lot #47. Eli was resident and forty acres had been improved; there was a frame house and barn; there were one hundred fifty fruit trees; and the property was *"first rate for all kinds of grain and fruit."* There is a note that *"the resident will see to it soon."* And, on September 10, 1829, Eli Webster renewed his contract.

According to the 1836 Holland Land Company map, landowners of Lot #47 included Sylvannus Crissey (one hundred fifteen acres), Alvin Crissey, and C. Warren. It appears that Sylvannus Crissey had two parts of Lot #47: (1.) east from Bear Lake to the end of Lot #47; and (2.) west from Bear Lake to the border with Lot #56 for 115 32/100 acres. The south east part of Lot #47 was held by Alvin Crissey and C. Warren.

The 1854 wall map shows landowners as J. Warren, C. Warren, C. Thompson, and M. Warren. The 1881 Chautauqua County Atlas mentions L.C. Warren (two hundred forty-one acres), Mrs. A. K. Warren (seventy-two acres), E. Bowen (one hundred seven and a third acres), and A. B. Lazell (one hundred seventy two acres)

LOTS #50 and 42 in the Town of Pomfret. On the northeast and northwest side of Bear Lake

LOT #50: In Barris' *Holland Land Company Delinquent Contracts,* Richard Kelley is listed as owner of one hundred fifty acres on parts of both Lot #50 (east side of lot) and Lot #42 (west side of lot). He purchased his contract for one hundred fifty acres on Lots #50 and #42 (Township 5, Range 12) on September 3, 1810. He was subsequently delinquent, but renewed his contract on February 9, 1830. His land is described as follows: *"Richard Kelley, resident; twenty-five acres improved on lot 42; frame house & barn, seventy-five fruit trees; maple, beach, cucumber & whiteash; good lot; pleasant situation"*[xxiii] This is the same Kelley whose family is described in Chapter 7.

According to Barris, Parley Munger signed a contract for eighty acres on December 7, 1817. It appears that contract was transferred to John Russel, but then Parley Munger renewed the contract on September 17, 1829. The property is described as follows: *"resident; twenty acres improved; log house & barn; fifty fruit trees; beach, maple &c steep western descent; strong soil for good for corn, grass."ˣˣⁱᵛ*

The 1836 Holland Land Company Map shows that John Martin owned two hundred thirty-nine acres of Lot #50. The 1854 wall map shows Sq. E. Kelly as owner of Lot # 50, and the 1881 Chautauqua County Atlas indicates the following landowners of Lot #50: J[ohn]. Cooper (one hundred eighty acres), G. Martin (ninety-nine and a half acres) and S. Turck (Turk) fifty acres. And, lastly, the 1916 map of Chautauqua lists the following as landowners of Lot #50: J. L. Sullivan (M. Dieter) seventy acres and George Cooper (one hundred ten acres). There is a narrow strip running north-west [perhaps Gilbert Drive?] and an arrow pointing to it saying "Coopers Summer Camps."

LOT # 42: Andrew Young mentions Richard Kelley as the owner of Lot #42 in June, 1814 (see above); and Parley Munger as owner of part of Lot #42 in July, 1819.ˣˣᵛ Young also indicates the following owners, without mentioning a date, of Lot #42 Bela Kelly and Reuben Munger; he also mentions owners in 1854 of Lot #42: B. Kelly, S. & E. Kelly, and P. Munger. P. Munger is also mentioned in the 1836 Holland Land Company Map as owner of Lot #42. E. Kelly is mentioned in the 1854 wall map as owner of Lot #42. And the *1881 Chautauqua County Atlas* indicates Kelly owned one hundred ninety-five acres in Lot #42, and J. Sullivan owned eighty-four and a half acres in Lot #42.

Finally, the 1916 map of Chautauqua County lists the following as landowners of Lot #42: "W.W.Mgr [?], up (Kelly Hill Road) J.N.G. Martin (one hundred ninety-one acres), O. J. Turk (one hundred twenty-six acres), N. Burg (eighty-six acres), Mrs. J. M. Kelley (one hundred sixty-seven acres), and E. J. Rossiter (ninety-five acres)."

APPENDIX C
MAPS

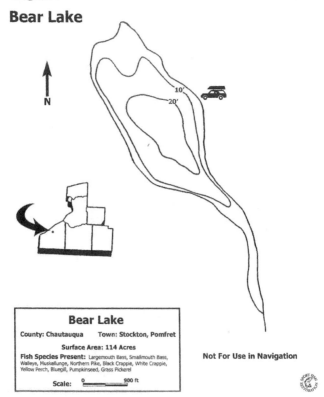

New York State Department of Environmental Conservation
Division of Fish, Wildlife and Marine Resources
Lake Map Series

Region 9

Bear Lake

10'
20'

N

Bear Lake

County: Chautauqua   Town: Stockton, Pomfret

Surface Area: 114 Acres

Fish Species Present: Largemouth Bass, Smallmouth Bass,
Walleye, Muskellunge, Northern Pike, Black Crappie, White Crappie,
Yellow Perch, Bluegill, Pumpkinseed, Grass Pickerel

Scale: 0   900 ft

Not For Use in Navigation

New York State Department of Environmental Conservation Division
of Fish, Wildlife & Marine Resources Lake Map Series, Region
9, Bear Lake

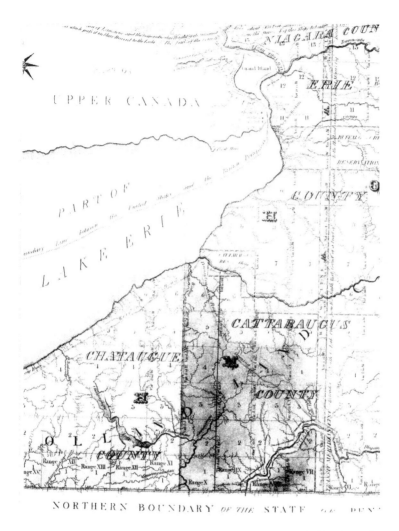

A map of the Morris Purchase, West Geneseo by the Holland Land Company, 1804, revised 1829 ("laid down from the actual survey" by Joseph & B. Ellicott, 1800)

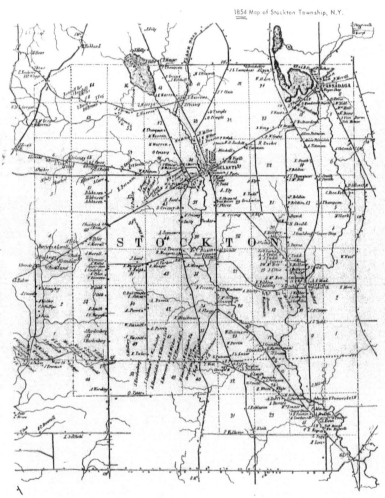

1854 Map of Stockton Township, N.Y.

Taken from the 1854 Wall Map of Chautauqua County, New York. Published by Collins G. Keeney; 15 Minor Street; Phila., Pa. - 1854. Copy furnished by Warren B. Cutting from his copy of this map. There is also a copy at the Chautauqua Co. Clerks Office, Mayville, N.Y. Reproduced by; Taddio Printing Co.; 77 Howard St.; Fredonia, N.Y., April 1979

Taken from the 1854 Wall Map of Chautauqua County, Published by
Collins G. Keeney, 15 Minor Street, Philadelphia, PA., 1854

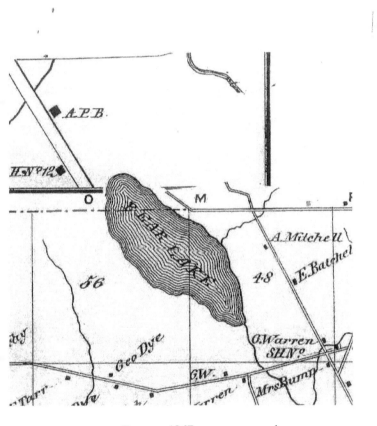

From an 1867 map; source unknown

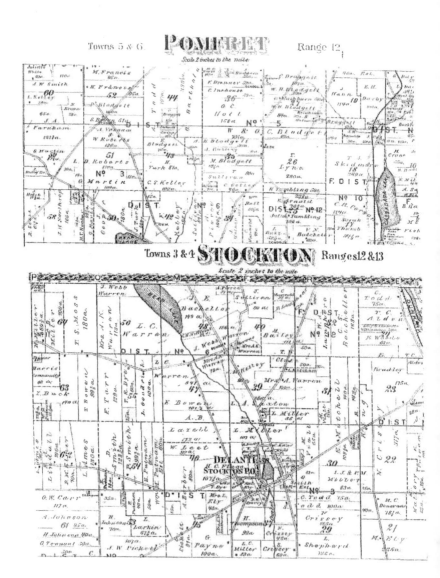

From the 1881 *Chautauqua County Atlas*; Shows Lots 50 and 42 in the Town of Pomfret and shows Lots 56, 48 & 47 in the Town of Stockton

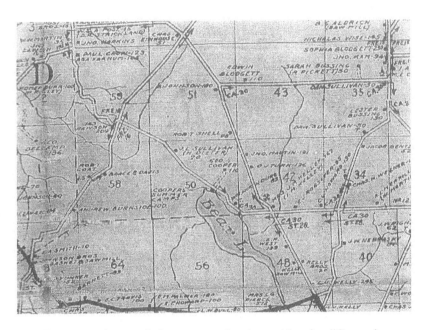

From an early twentieth century undated map (showing "Cooper's Summer Camps," Turk or Sodom Road and the James Rawson's residence)

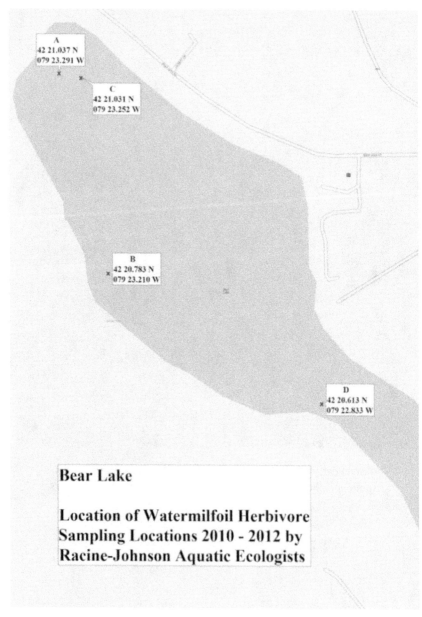

A
42 21.037 N
079 23.291 W

C
42 21.031 N
079 23.252 W

B
42 20.783 N
079 23.210 W

D
42 20.613 N
079 22.833 W

Bear Lake

Location of Watermilfoil Herbivore Sampling Locations 2010 - 2012 by Racine-Johnson Aquatic Ecologists

Locations of points A-D where weevils and moths were put into Bear Lake as part of the bio control program

MAPS

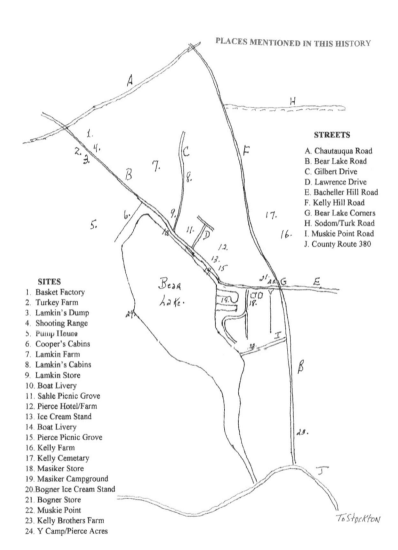

PLACES MENTIONED IN THIS HISTORY

STREETS

A. Chautauqua Road
B. Bear Lake Road
C. Gilbert Drive
D. Lawrence Drive
E. Bacheller Hill Road
F. Kelly Hill Road
G. Bear Lake Corners
H. Sodom/Turk Road
I. Muskie Point Road
J. County Route 380

SITES

1. Basket Factory
2. Turkey Farm
3. Lamkin's Dump
4. Shooting Range
5. Pump House
6. Cooper's Cabins
7. Lamkin Farm
8. Lamkin's Cabins
9. Lamkin Store
10. Boat Livery
11. Sahle Picnic Grove
12. Pierce Hotel/Farm
13. Ice Cream Stand
14. Boat Livery
15. Pierce Picnic Grove
16. Kelly Farm
17. Kelly Cemetary
18. Masiker Store
19. Masiker Campground
20. Bogner Ice Cream Stand
21. Bogner Store
22. Muskie Point
23. Kelly Brothers Farm
24. Y Camp/Pierce Acres

Streets and Sites at Bear Lake, 2017

BIBLIOGRAPHY

Barden, Virginia Washburn. *Holland Land Company Earliest Sales in Chautauqua County New York*. (Chautauqua County Genealogical Society, 1990).

Barris, Lois. *Holland Land Company Delinquent Contracts in Chautauqua County, New York*. (Chautauqua County Genealogical Society, 1991).

Berndt, Cathryn. *Stockton: Seen Through the Rear View Mirror*. (Dunkirk, New York: Woloszyn Printery, 1988).

Crocker, Elizabeth L. *Yesterdays In and Around Pomfret*, 5 vols. 1954–1959.

Cutter, William B. *Genealogical and Family History in Western New York*. 3 vols. (1912).

Downs, John P. *History of Chautauqua County and Its People*, 3 vols. (Boston:American Historical Society, 1921).

Edson, Obed. *History of Chautauqua County, New York*. Georgia D.Merrill, ed. 2 vols. (Boston:W.A.Fergusson & Company, 1894).

Livsey, Karen E. *Western New York Land Transactions 1804-1824* (1991); *Western New York Land Transactions 1825-1835*.

McMahon, Helen G. *Chautauqua County, A History*. (Buffalo: Henry Stewart, 1958).

Morrison, William. *Chautauqua County History*. (1874).

215

Palmer, Joseph W. *A Guide to Local History, Oral History, Audiovisual Histories in Public Libraries and Historical Societies in Cattauraugus and Chautauqua Counties, New York.* (Cornell University Library, 1982. A revised version was published by the School of Information & Library Studies, SUNY Buffalo, 1985).

Piersons, Helen [Town of Stockton Historian]. *Septquicentennial Memory Book, 1821-1996.*

Smith, John & Ruth. *They were Here: On the Trail of our Indian Pioneers.* (Jamestown, NY: Copy Quick, 1990).

[Souvenir Program]. *Town of Stockton: Old Fashioned Days, September 12 & 13, 1992*

Stewart, William. *New Topographical Atlas of Chautauqua County.* (New York, 1867).

[Stockton Town Picnic Programs]. Nos. 3 (1900), 37 (1934), 38 (1935), 39 (1936), 41 (1938), 42 (1939), 47 (1944), 49 (1946), 52 (1949), 53 (1950), 56 (1953), 57 (1954), 58 (1955), 59 (1956), 58 (1955), 59 (1956), 60 (1957), 61 (1958), 62 (1959)

Turner, Orsamus. *Pioneer History of the Holland Purchase of Western New York.* (1849; reprinted 1974).

Vanderlaan, Stanley G. *Oddes and Ends: Archaeological Memories*, 4th edition. [2008]

Warren, Emory F. *Sketches of the History of Chautauqua County.* (Jamestown: J.W. Fletcher, 1846).

Young, Andrew. *History of Chautauqua County, New York from its First Settlement to the Present Time.* (Buffalo: Matthews & Warren, 1875).

ENDNOTES

i.   The websites of the Roger Tory Peterson Institute of Natural History and the New York State Department of Environmental Conservation. Jeff Tome. "Glacial Bulldozer Leaves Lakes Behind. *Jamestown Post Journal* (19 August 2012).

ii.   Obed Edson. *History of Chautauqua County Anterior to its Pioneer Settlement* (New York, 1894).

iii.   Helen G. McMahon. *Chautauqua County, A History*. (Buffalo: Henry Stewart, 1958), p. 11 iv. McMahon, 12.

v.   Quoted in Orsamus Turner. *Pioneer History of the Holland Purchase of Western New York*. (1849). reprinted 1974, 20.

vi.   Stanley G. Vanderlaan. *Odds and Ends: Archaeological Memoirs*, 4th Editon.

vii.   Obed, 150-151.

viii.   Chapter LXXV in Edson's *History*, 895ff.

ix.   Virginia Washburn Barden. *Holland Land Company Earliest Sales in Chautauqua County New York*. (Chautauqua County Genealogical Society, 1990). 69.

x.   http://app.chautauquacounty.com/hist_struct/Pomfret/131CenterPomfret2.html

xi.   http://chautgen.org/pastMembers.php

xii.   Barden, p. 69

xiii.   Barden, p. 5.

xiv.   John P. Downs, ed. *Chautauqua County and Its People*. (1921)

xv.   Andrew Young. *History of Chautauqua County*. (1875), AY 556.

xvi.   Lois Barris. *Holland Land Company Delinguent Contracts in Chautauqua County New York*. (Chautauqua County Genealogical Society), 1991

xvii.   Barris, p. 102.

xviii. The Holland Land Company map indicates the earliest deed land (before 1836). That map is generally not available to the public.

xix. Edson, AY 563

xx . Edson, AY 556

xxi. Barris, p. 5

xxii. Barris, p. 47.

xxiii. Barris, p. 72

xxiv. Barris, p. 89

xxv. Young, AY 467.

INDEX

Note: *m* indicates a map; *p*, a photograph